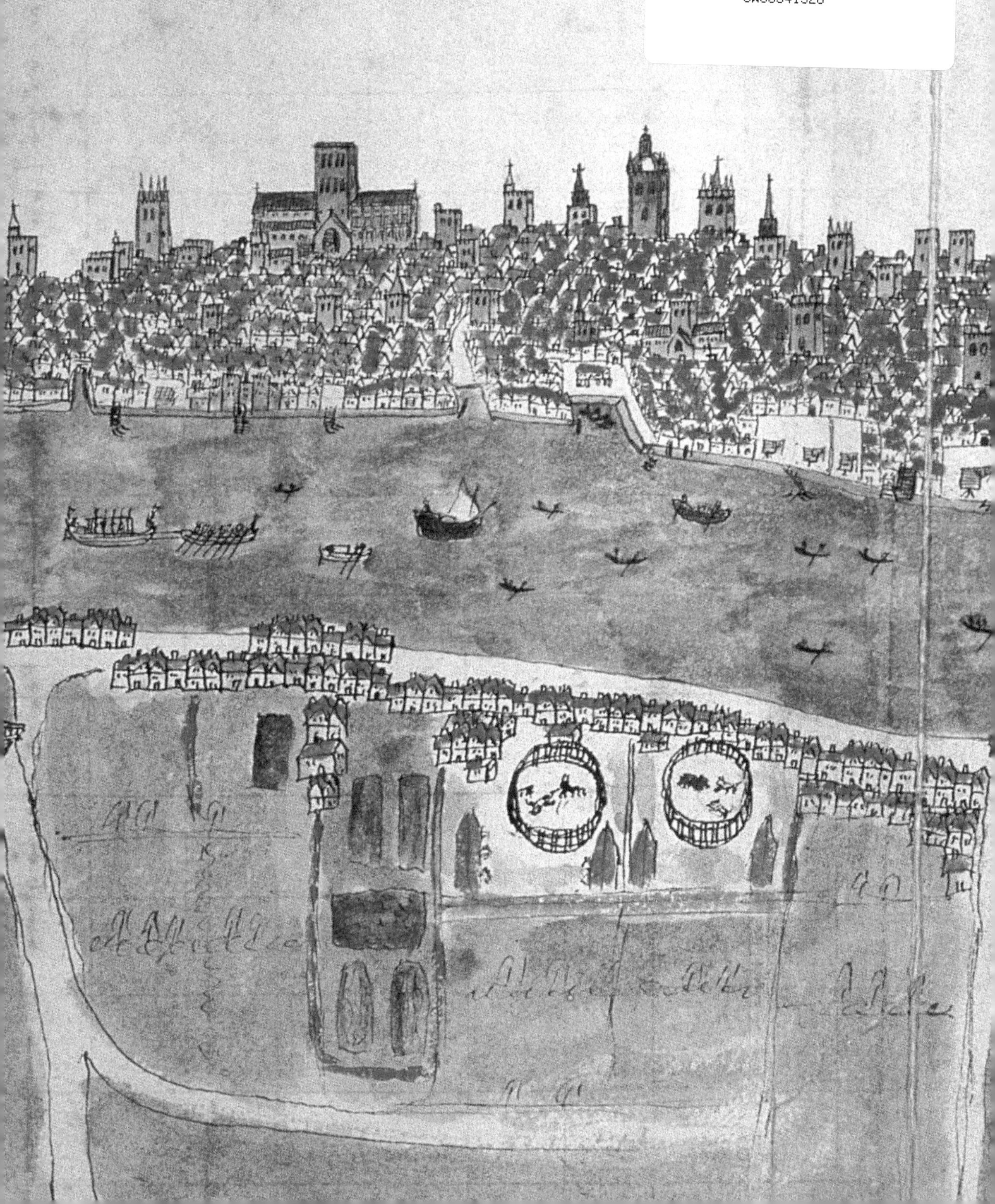
LONDON.

HENRY SMITH
His Life & Legacy

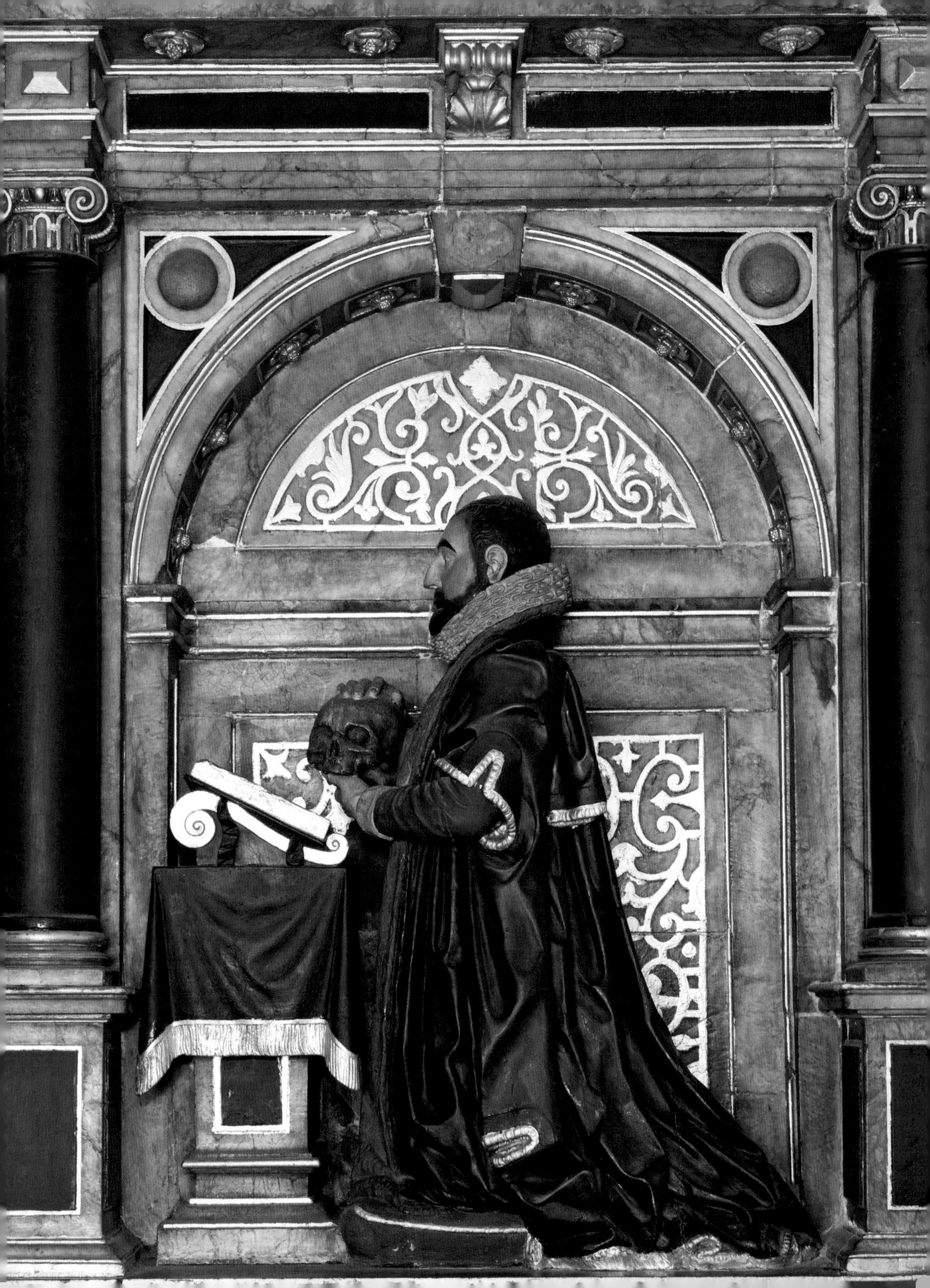

Lucy Lethbridge & Tim Wales

HENRY SMITH

His Life & Legacy

THE HENRY SMITH CHARITY

Frontispiece: Henry Smith's memorial in All Saints Church, Wandsworth

The map reproduced on the endpapers shows London in 1588,
at the time when Henry had established himself as a prosperous iron merchant.

First published in Great Britain 2015
by The Henry Smith Charity
6th Floor
65 Leadenhall Street
London EC3A 2AD

A CIP catalogue record for this book is available from the British Library.

ISBN 978 0 9930945 0 7

Picture editor: Julia Brown
Designed and produced by Simon Haviland
Typeset in Monotype Bell
Printed and bound in Great Britain by Information Press, Eynsham, Oxford

Contents

Acknowledgements

This project was the brainchild of Amelia Fitzalan Howard of the Henry Smith Charity and its completion owes everything to her unflagging enthusiasm and encouragement. We are also grateful for the great support and interest of Richard Hopgood, Noel Manns, Nick Acland, James Hambro, Brian McGeough, Merlyn Lowther, James Hordern and Gordon Lee-Steere.

The creation of the book was the result of teamwork. It was made possible by the patient vision, skills and experience of Simon Haviland combined with the flair and expertise of Julia Brown: they transformed a plain text into a richly illustrated book that was still further enhanced by Dr John Crook's wonderful photographs. The researches of Edward Peacock into the charity's archives were an invaluable source of information and ideas. Our thanks, too, to Jenny Haviland for her immaculate proofreading, to Robert O'Rorke for patiently printing out our pages and to Vicki Robinson for compiling the index.

We are also indebted for their help to Richard and Diana Lethbridge, Julian Pooley of the Surrey History Centre, Isabel Hernandez of Kensington Library, David Luck of London Metropolitan Archives, Gillian Barnes-Riding of the Surrey Heath Museum and the librarians at the Wandsworth Heritage Service. Thanks also go to Dr David Bartle of the Haberdashers' Company; Katie George of the Salters' Company; Robert Noel, Lancaster Herald; Crestina Forcina of the Wellcome Library; Charles Hind and Vicky Wilson of the RIBA Drawings Collection; Elizabeth Taylor of the National Portrait Gallery; Siān Phillips of The Bridgeman Art Library; Pedro Lopez-Pelegrin of Peter Harrington Books; Andrew Barton, Oliver Harwood and Angela Locke of RH & RW Clutton; and Jane Snowden of Wandsworth parish. We are grateful to Mrs Dennis Flanders for permission to reproduce her late husband's depiction of Silver Street.

Many people gave their time and knowledge to the project – including Gail Tendler, Matthew Gill, Jennie Long and Jo Marren-King of the Henry Smith Charity. Thanks are also due to Brendan Walsh, Peter Crook, Maggie Hill, Deirdre Munro, Sally-Anne Greenfield of Leeds Community Foundation, Sara Gowen of Sheffield Homestart, John Redwood of L'Arche Edinburgh, Zaiba Qureshi of Housing for Women, Kate Bratt-Farrar of Leeds Women's Aid, Liza Kellett of the Community Foundation in Wales – and to Trevor, Christine, Vicky and John at the Pencader Family Centre.

And without Lucy Hannah this book would never have happened at all.

Lucy Lethbridge

Foreword

Henry Smith's lifetime and legacy is surprisingly poorly recorded. Lucy Lethbridge and Tim Wales have now dug deep to unearth an intriguing story of his career and his achievements, which in many ways were typical of a successful man of business in the city of London in the early seventeenth century.

Henry had a Christian ethic, a sense of family duty, even though he had no children of his own, and a shrewd financial brain at a time when conventional banks did not exist and money was lent on a private basis. He spent much time in his latter years thinking about the charity which he endowed and how it should operate. His choice in the appointment of the early trustees is interesting – several owed Smith substantial amounts of money making their motives perhaps somewhat conflicted. This led, in the early years after Henry's death, to various claims and counterclaims of malfeasance. The result was a ruling that trustee appointments were to be scrutinised by the Archbishop of Canterbury – still the case today – and the Lord Chancellor. Little did these early trustees realise how significant in the charity's history would the purchase from one of their number, Sir William Blake, soon after Henry's death of eighty-five acres in the village of Brompton prove to be.

In the time that I have had the privilege to be a trustee, the world of grant-making has changed out of all recognition and Henry Smith's charity has adapted to meet the needs of twenty-first century Britain. While moving with the times we still preserve and take pride in our history and traditions. In accordance with the terms of the founder's will, we still assist his descendants and help clergy in need, and we still even own some of the farms which were purchased by Henry himself in the seventeenth century. The size of the endowment, however, has increased hugely and now allows the trustees to distribute over £100 million every four years to a wide range of causes, mostly those with little public appeal, by supporting many small charities which have difficulty raising funding elsewhere.

Although the sums have grown, the core values of the Henry Smith Charity remain unchanged. Lucy and Tim have diligently researched and compiled a fascinating account, which has come from a wide variety of sources and will stand as a record to be enjoyed by future generations.

James Hambro
Chairman, The Henry Smith Charity

HENRY SMITH'S FAMILY TREE OVER SIX GENERATIONS

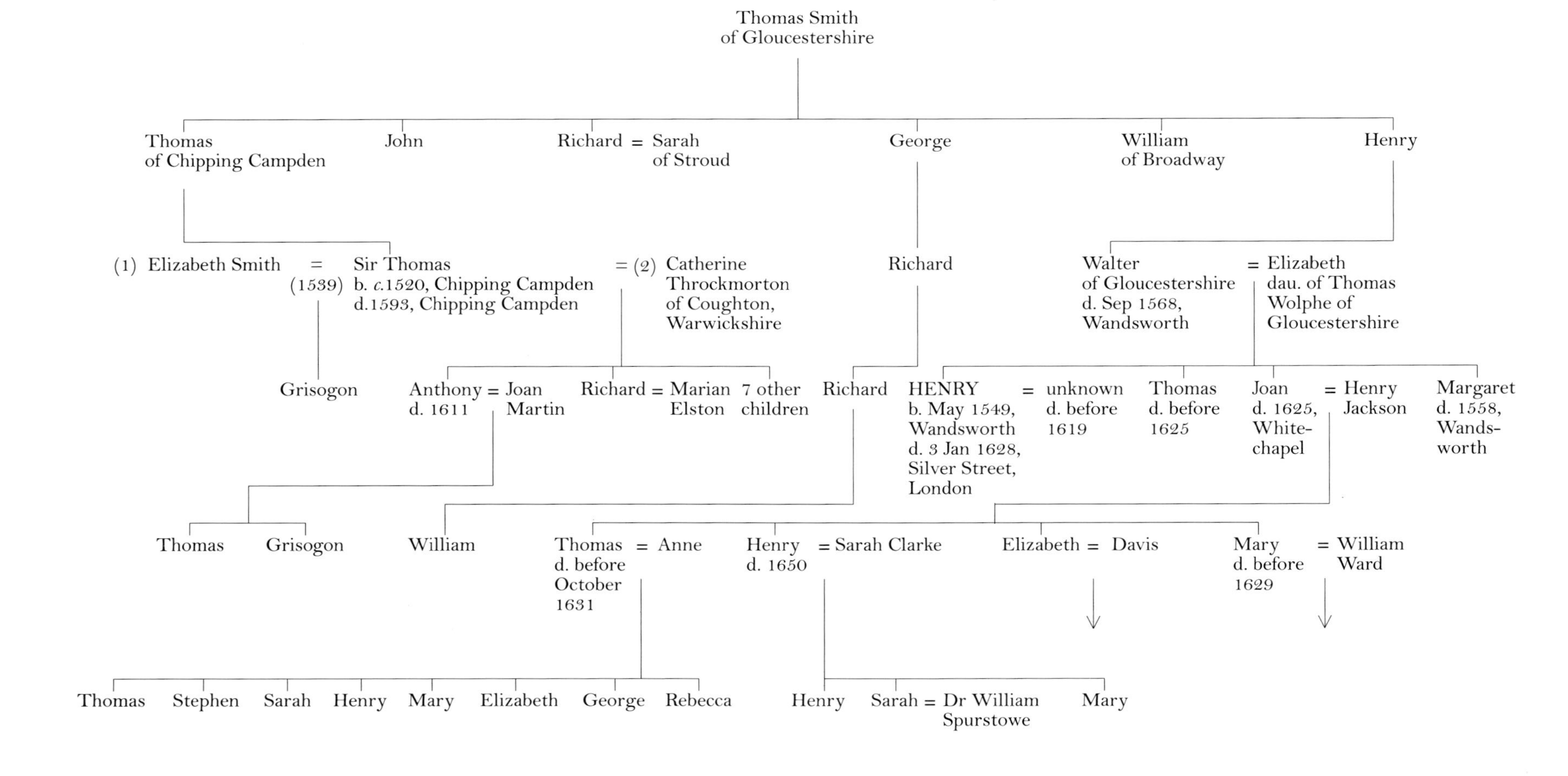

Introduction

Four centuries after it was first established, the Henry Smith Charity is one of the largest grant-making charities in Britain: in 2013, it gave away £27 million. The recipients of Henry Smith's benefaction in a new millennium are both more wide-ranging and more specific than their founder could ever have envisaged when he made his will in 1628. They include the disabled, prisoners and ex-offenders, the homeless, asylum seekers and refugees, children and young people and those in addiction rehabilitation schemes.

Yet Smith's philanthropic legacy has been maintained over the years with a remarkable degree both of consistency and continuity: indeed it would require the intervention of Parliament to overturn the terms under which a charity established by a deed operates. So because, in 1628, Smith left money for the welfare of needy descendants of his sister, Joan, known as the 'poor kindred', the charity today still sees to it that this benefaction is honoured – with nearly 6,000 proven kindred registered. Smith's legacy to 'poor clergy' also continues, with grants administered by dioceses on behalf of the charity. Even the money he left for 'the redemption of the captives of Barbary pirates' has found a contemporary form in the grants given to help trafficked women – a modern form of slavery.

Most striking of all in its longevity, however, is the continued practice of awarding the annual grants to allocated parishes (nearly 200 of them, including every parish in Surrey) – as laid out by Henry Smith in his will and then formalised by the trustees he selected. No detail was overlooked in the will as to how these grants would be administered by a local body of trustees, who would award the money to parishioners considered in need. For 300 years it was mainly received in the form of bread, fuel or clothing: nowadays it may well constitute help with travel expenses or school trips.

The ongoing success of Henry Smith's charity is largely due to its founder's astute foresight and understanding of the value of land. The charity's vast estates have been the foundation of its income since the seventeenth century. Born in 1549, Smith was one of those who made fortunes in the great land grab that followed the dissolution of the monasteries, receiving property and estates in exchange for debts in a variety of ingenious negotiations; by the 1620s, he was the owner of thousands of acres and the mortgagee of thousands more. It was however after his death that his trustees were to make the most important acquisition on behalf of the charity: the purchase during the 1640s of a marshy estate of eighty-five acres situated just outside London, in the parish of Kensington.

For a century and a half the village of Brompton was a quiet rural backwater occupied mainly by market gardens; then, in a matter of a few decades, it was swept up in the huge nineteenth-century development of west London, becoming the expensive residential area of crescents, squares and terraces that it is today. He could not have known it at the time, but the moment that Sir William Blake signed over his estate to the trustees of Smith's Charity for £2,000 he can be said to have firmly secured the charity's legacy into the twenty-first century.

So who exactly was Henry Smith? Over the years a startling variety of myths and misinformation have clustered like barnacles on a few shreds of evidence. In some chronicles Smith had been described as a salt merchant, in others he was a silversmith; in one nineteenth-century account, he was reported to have himself been a captive of Moorish pirates. The most persistent myth of all was the wildest: that Henry Smith was one and the same as a character known as 'Dog Smith', who, dressed as a vagrant, wandered rural Surrey and bestowed his largesse where the locals treated his dog with respect. It seemed that the blankness of Henry Smith's identity was a sheet on which any desirable or colourful image could be imprinted.

When we began our researches into Henry's* life, we had therefore very few clues to guide us. His dates were 1549 to 1628, so we could pin his life to the Elizabethan and Jacobean ages right up to the reign of Charles I. We had a few other scraps of information: the records showed that he had been a member of the Salters' Company; he had a sister, Joan Jackson; he lived in Silver Street in the city of London; he was born in Wandsworth; and at the time of his death, he was the possessor of a vast fortune. Apart from a brief if hyperbolic mention in Thomas Fuller's 1662 *Worthies of England* (where he is described as a 'whale' of philanthropic virtue), Henry appears in no published works of his time. The three main sources for our research were his monument, his will and the lives of the trustees that he had chosen to lead the charity in the years after his death.

Smith's monument in All Saints Church, Wandsworth, on which a bearded figure in alderman's garb gazes expressionless at a skull, has a panel beneath it that recites conventional seventeenth-century pieties about civic virtue and charitable endeavours. His family tree is elaborately espaliered with grand armorial connections but there is no hint as to the origins of his fortune (somewhat murky) or even the identity of his wife.

Henry's will, which runs to many pages, revealed on first reading a conventional interest in the kind of charitable causes that were encompassed by the 1601 Act of Charitable Uses: chiefly the relief of poverty for those 'deserving' (Henry took a strong line on whoremongers, pilferers and swearers); even the benefaction for the redemption of captives was among those causes recommended by the 1601 Act. It was reading between the lines of the will that began to reveal tiny glimpses of the man himself as an individual. We detected a hint of the micro-manager in his determination to keep the charity operating entirely under its own guidelines rather than, in the more conventional manner, bequeathing it to be run by his livery company. Then there was the passing mention of Dorchester, a Calvinist centre, and the sum bequeathed for the promulgation of the Gospels: not perhaps definitive evidence of a religious conviction but they are certainly suggestive of an inclination towards Puritanism. His concern for the descendants of his sister, Joan Jackson, also intrigued us; all the evidence was that the Jacksons were prosperous – had something happened in Henry's life that had brought home to him how quickly fortunes could change and leave future generations in need?

An examination of the lives of those who surrounded him also provided many insights, in fact gave Henry's life the vital definition we needed for a picture of the man himself. Through court cases, complicated property transactions and the interlocking lives with richer documentation than Henry's, we built up a picture of his world, the circles he moved in. We found the name of Henry Smith, trader, usurer, speculator, popping up in unlikely places, a man with his fingers in many business pies. The cast of Henry's inner circle changed regularly, with trusted cohorts being expelled, new ones admitted, and the old ones sometimes allowed back into the fold again.

* We have referred to Henry Smith throughout the book as Henry. This is not due to over-familiarity but simply because with so many Smiths in his story it was the easiest way to identify him.

Documents from the Henry Smith Charity archive, the earliest dating back to 1631.

The first trustees, the men who can be said to have laid the foundations for the Henry Smith Charity today, were also men of business, their tangled network of debts and deals and alliances underpinning the first fortunes of the charity; almost every one of them owed Henry money. Beyond this, these men exhibited a wide and likeable human variety: some were Puritans; some had Catholic sympathies; two were avid Royalists; several were Parliamentarians; most pragmatically swung between the two. Among their number were one or two moneylending chancers, several city dignitaries, a hopeless spendthrift, a lawyer, a judge and a soldier.

From the snippets that our researches revealed we found a man absolutely of his time: Henry Smith was a self-made tycoon from a respectable landowning family that had gone down in the world; a shrewd and often ruthless businessman, a moneylender and a property speculator, he was a man of the City as it flourished into a European financial centre.

Most importantly, one of the few things we can know for certain about Henry is that he was obsessively concerned with his legacy. All the evidence tells us that he spent his last years in the 1620s working out to the last minute detail how his charity would be run, where the money would be spent, how its giving would be administered and who would be qualified to receive it. He was not to know then that the Henry Smith Charity would travel so successfully into the twenty-first century, translating its founder's aims for a new millennium. But we do not need to know everything about the man to be sure that the triumphant survival of his great foundation would give him the greatest of satisfaction.

Lucy Lethbridge
London, September 2014

A plan of London from *Civitates Orbis Terrarum*, 1572, by Franz Hogenberg (detail). Wandsworth was still a distant riverside village to the west of the city.

1

Wandsworth

Henry Smith was born in Wandsworth, just outside London, some time in May 1549, during the short reign of King Edward VI. The years around 1549 were riven by events that were to profoundly influence Henry's life and the future of his charity: the dissolution of the monasteries in the 1530s followed by the Crown's need to raise money for expensive wars abroad had released thousands of acres of land on to the market; and the creation of a Protestant church had seen the destruction of a huge framework of traditional charitable organisations at parish level.

Life in Wandsworth and its surrounding villages in northern Surrey had changed dramatically over the course of a few decades. The parish had once constituted a part of the Battersea lands that were granted to the abbots of Westminster by William the Conqueror. The dissolution of Merton Priory in Wimbledon in 1538 had an effect on all the villages in the region, most of which had been linked to, or been dependent on, the Augustinians at Merton. The monastic estate was dissolved in 1540, just nine years before Henry's birth, and its component parts were rapidly scooped up for development by courtiers, prosperous merchants and people of fashion who required property close to the court and the capital. Nearby Wimbledon, comprising just forty-six dwellings, had recently been transformed by the Cecil family, who had built a large palace there. Down the river lay the royal palaces of Richmond and Hampton Court, the latter built for Cardinal Wolsey; Henry VIII's magnificent palace of Nonsuch had been erected not far away in Cheam, using the stones of Merton Priory; after the fall of Wolsey, Thomas Cromwell, one of the chief architects of the English reformation – and himself born in Putney – bought the Manor of Wimbledon in 1546.

The expansion of London had brought prosperity and influence to the region. King Henry VIII stopped in Wandsworth on his way to Nonsuch just before his death in 1547. Desperately ill, his legs covered in ulcers and suffering from debilitating constipation, he was then forced to stay a whole week at the manor house in Wimbledon that had been owned since 1544 by his queen, Catherine Parr.

The River Wandle, on which Wandsworth, or 'Wandlesworth', as it was originally known, is situated, is a tributary of the Thames and had for centuries supported a thriving industry of watermills. The Wandle's unusually rapid fall (124 feet in nine miles) and its fast-flowing waters made it ideal for driving mill wheels; unlike the Thames, it never froze during the winter months. Earlier generations had referred to the river as the Lutbourne, a variation of the Anglo-Saxon *hlida burnan* – meaning loud or fast-flowing – and the Domesday Book records in 1086 that there were at least thirteen corn mills on the Wandle. These mills were used for grinding corn and meal but the river was also one of the major national centres for treating the wool that was England's most important export. 'Fulling' describes the process of using running water to clean and scour the oiliness out of sheepskins and a key ingredient of this process was fuller's earth, which was plentiful

A later view of Wandsworth in an engaving by Jean Baptiste Claude Chatelain (1710–58) showing the watermills still proliferating on the banks of the Wandle.

in Surrey. There were a great number of fulling mills situated along the Wandle at the time of Henry Smith's birth.

Wandsworth and its mills had also become an important centre of the lucrative English textile dyeing industry. By the eighteenth century, Alexander Pope would describe the clear waters of 'the blue, transparent Vandalis' but two hundred years before that, the River Wandle would regularly have run red with the crimson dye, made from Brazil wood, madder or (later) scarlet, that was milled along the river. The celebrated Wandsworth scarlet was reputed to be the only red that did not run in the rain and was therefore much in demand for the red hats of Roman cardinals.

Wandsworth was affected, too, by the religious turbulence of the mid sixteenth century. In 1539, the parish priest John Griffiths and his curate were hanged, drawn and quartered at St Thomas à Waterings for resisting the new religious ordinances. The churchwardens' accounts at All Saints, Wandsworth – those still surviving begin in 1545 – record the changes that the parish and its worship underwent as England lurched from reformation to counter-reformation and back again in the space of two decades. The account books show that new service books in English were purchased in the early 1540s and also a communion table to replace the stone altar – and the removal of the altar and thirteen wooden and alabaster images had to be paid for. In 1546, there was a payment for 'one new book called the Paraphrases of Erasmus'. And 'for taking down the rood loft and making the same in plain.' In 1552–3, Queen Mary I having acceded to the throne, Catholic liturgical elements were hastily returned to comply with new rules: another 'communion book' had to be purchased and a 'holy water sprinkle'. Among the other features of the parish that disappeared with the Reformation (never to return) was a hermitage with a resident hermit – probably attached to Westminster Abbey. In 1524, the sum of fourpence was reported to have been paid to 'the hermit of Wandsworth' on behalf of a nobleman travelling through Surrey.

Henry Smith was the son of Walter Smith and his wife, Elizabeth. How they had first arrived in Wandsworth is not known – for they both came from Gloucestershire families. Henry's sense of the importance of lineage is recorded in the coat of arms displayed on his elaborate wall monument in All Saints, the old parish church of Wandsworth, where he was buried. These lay claim to descent from the Smiths of Chipping Campden. The quarterings on Henry's

A detail from Henry Smith's memorial in Wandsworth. The wolves' heads are punning allusions to his mother's family, the Wolphes.

arms are the arms of that family, whilst other addi tions reflect further aspects of his family history. An eighteenth-century transcript of the herald's visitation of Gloucestershire for 1569 in the hand of the antiquarian Barak Longmate confirms Henry's claim to gentility. Henry's grandfather (also Henry) was the sixth son of Thomas Smith of Chipping Campden. Henry's mother, Elizabeth, was the daughter of Thomas Wolphe of Gloucestershire: hence the punning wolves' heads on the coat of arms.[1]

The Smiths, according to the researches of Charles Perkins Gwilt in the early nineteenth century, had been settled at Campden since at least the mid fourteenth century and claimed descent from Henry le Smythe, who in 1346 was recorded as owning property in Quenton (or Quinton), a village seven miles from Campden. By the time of the herald's visitation of Gloucestershire in 1532–3, one Thomas Smith was established in Campden as a wealthy landowner: this was either Walter Smith's grandfather or his uncle. The family flourished further with the third Thomas to succeed in the senior branch of the family, first cousin of Henry's father.

Thomas Smith plays an important part in the history of Henry Smith. He was a man of some distinction, someone with whom a self-made man might be proud to claim kinship; their relation is given further credence by the many business connections that Henry and the trustees of his charity were to have in later years with relatives and descendants of the Chipping Campden Smiths. Thomas spent his early years as a courtier in the court of King Henry VIII. Born around 1520, he became a Page of the Chamber and his name appears in the Privy Purse expenses of 1531 as receiving £10 per annum and his apparel. He attended the king in Calais in 1532, when he travelled there with Anne Boleyn to try and gain approval from Francis I for his attempts to have his marriage to Catherine of Aragon annulled. In 1544, Thomas was with Henry VIII at the siege of Boulogne; it was there that he received a grant of arms. Thomas retired from the court on the death of Henry VIII and thereafter occupied himself with local affairs in Gloucestershire, acting as a Justice of the Peace, a member of the Council of the Marches and High Sheriff in 1571 and 1583. He died in 1593 and is buried in St James's church, Chipping Campden, where a fine tomb depicts him with his wives and his numerous children.

Sir Thomas Smith married twice: in 1539 to (confusingly) Elizabeth Smith, a widow, with whom he had five children, including one surviving daughter, Grisogon, who was to inherit the manor of Campden on his death. After the death of Elizabeth, Thomas married Catherine, the daughter of Sir George Throckmorton of Coughton in Warwickshire, a prominent Catholic statesman. Catherine was the widow of Robert Winter of Worcestershire. (The Winters were also prominent Catholics: two Winters, nephews of Catherine's husband, were among those who took part in the Gunpowder Plot.) By Catherine, Thomas had nine children. His eldest son, Anthony Smith, was later to become a business associate of Sir William Bond, who in turn was an associate of Anthony's cousin Henry in London. In 1600 Anthony purchased the manor of Campden from his half-sister, Grisogon.

Henry Smith's connection to the Smiths of Campden may also have been an important one in the history of Smith's Charity. When it came to appointing the first trustees of his charity, eleven of the eighteen men Henry chose had direct connections with the Smiths of Campden, or more particularly with the Throckmortons, who were linked with some of the most influential families in the country. This may have been coincidence, reflecting a not uncommon entwining of families through marriage and kinship whose significance for individuals is less than it might appear on paper. Yet these relationships would have provided fruitful networks for someone who was to make his fortune lending money to impoverished members of the English nobility.

Walter Smith, as the son of a sixth son, was the scion of a less prosperous branch of the Smiths but nonetheless, during the 1540s, the tax records for Wandsworth show that Walter Smith (sometimes written as Smyth) was the parish's second highest taxpayer in 1547 (with an assessment of £25 and fifty shillings – which included subsidy payments on landholdings as well as goods) and joint second in 1549. There are also several references to Walter in the Wandsworth churchwardens' accounts. In 1547, for example, we learn that he rented most of the land belonging to the church, paying the parish £1 13s 4d in annual rent 'Due on Lady Saint Mary' (Lady Day, 25 March); in 1549, Walter paid for a year's rent of the 'Oziers' (willows), lying between Frying Pan Creek and the mouth of the Wandle.

Henry was Walter's eldest son and he had a sister Joan (of whom more later) and also a brother called Thomas – though we know nothing more about him than his name and that he must have predeceased his siblings. We do not know how many more of the Smiths' children died in infancy – but in 1558, the parish made a payment to Walter 'for the waste off two tapers at the burial of his daughter Margaret' (dripped wax was used to make new candles). Survival into adulthood in the sixteenth century was tenuous and daily life was fraught with dangers: the burial records of Wandsworth are full of children who drowned in a mill race; there were also several outbreaks of plague there during the period of Henry's growing up.

Walter died in September 1568 – leaving no will. At the time of his death he owned two watermills in Wandsworth but was also (according to his widow) 'heavily encumbered' with debts. His death precipitated a lawsuit in Chancery between Elizabeth and one of Walter's creditors, the Londoner Robert Kinge, a member of the Fishmongers' Company. And it is in the proceedings of this case that we catch our first glimpse of Henry Smith – then 20 years old.

According to Elizabeth Smith's Bill of Complaint, directed to Sir Nicholas Bacon, the Lord Keeper, Walter Smyth and Bartholomew Mathewe had borrowed £20 from Robert Kinge. To secure the debt, Smith and Mathewe bound themselves on 28 November 1567 for double the amount of the debt (a standard practice), should it not be repaid on 24 July following. But Smith and his co-debtor failed to repay on the due date; the bond was forfeit and Kinge foreclosed, obtaining a writ of extent by which Smith's lands and

The tomb of Sir Thomas Smith in St James's Church, Chipping Campden. The children of his two marriages are depicted below him.

goods were forfeited to allow the recovery of the debt. Smith approached Kinge and a compromise was agreed upon, on 7 September 1568, before the under-sheriff of Surrey: if Smith would pay Kinge £30 within a fortnight he would remit the forfeiture. However, Smith was dead within the month, having managed only to give Kinge's wife £12 in part payment.

Immediately, Kinge claimed possession of Walter's watermills. Elizabeth, who had been granted administration of her late husband's estate, took possession of them, telling the court that her son Henry, his father's natural heir, had made over the mills to her for her lifetime. They were, she said, to enable her to pay off Walter's debts and to provide for her

The Gunpowder Plot conspirators. Engraving, 1606. Sir Thomas Smith's second wife was Catherine Throckmorton, whose first husband was Robert Winter of Warwickshire. The Winters were prominent Catholics – and two of them were plotters.

upkeep because Walter had left her in penury. She put up a good case:

> And afterwards in September last Walter Smith died intestate, after whose death the mills descended to Henry Smith as Walter's son and heir, and the administration of Walter's goods and chattels also was committed to your oratrix. And for that Walter was greatly indebted at the time of his death and that his goods and chattels would not by a great sum pay his debts and also for your poor oratrix's relief, having been left nothing by her husband towards her relief and comfort, Henry granted to her the watermills to have until such time as Walter's whole debts should be paid off. By reason whereof she entered into the premises, and has occupied and taken the profits of them since Walter's death.

Elizabeth went on to claim that although Kinge had 'the £12 in his hands', and has been offered a further £18, yet he was refusing either to accept the latter sum or pay back the £12. Kinge had rejected a compromise repayment allegedly agreed upon shortly before Walter's death, but rather was insisting upon the amount due under the original bond – with a further £12 costs tagged on. He had sued her under the bond, and had her ejected from the watermills. Kinge responded by denying Elizabeth's right to the watermills: Henry had not – and could not – grant her them (and given Henry's age this was probably true). Walter had given him £12 but only as part of the payment due under the recognizance: he demanded only the return of the £40 plus costs. Elizabeth in her turn made a final offer, which Kinge was forced to accept, of £30 on top of the £12 already paid: she considered £42 sufficient recompense for the forbearing of £20 for three months.[2]

This early exposure to the complexities of moneylending will have taught Henry some valuable and bitter lessons.

2

London

The next forty years of Henry's life and employment are only intermittently illuminated. At some time between 1568, when we first encountered him, and the early years of the seventeenth century, he must have married. We know of the existence of his wife only from this entry in the records of the College of Arms at the time of his burial: 'He married only one wife, who died long since, but never had any issue by her.' Of his wife's name, or of her family, we know nothing.

That Henry was a member of the Salters' Company is one of the few established facts about him – and it has given rise to the understandable but confusing report in some later accounts that he had made his fortune working as a salt merchant. The Salters were listed tenth among what are today known as the Great Twelve companies, a hierarchy of wealth, status and influence that was at that time topped by the Mercers and tailed by the Vintners. In the livery companies' hands, wrote John Stow, the tallow-chandler, antiquarian and author of the 1593 *Survey of London*, 'was held most of the riches of the city'.

Every aspect of London life in the sixteenth century was affected by the companies. They regulated, trained and traded, and as major landlords had a stranglehold on properties and rents. The Merchant Taylors were the last word in cloth measuring, the Grocers controlled the import of spices and drugs and the Haberdashers had the monopoly on pin manufacture, making and selling hats and importing luxury goods from Italy. The regulations that underpinned working life in London were maintained by the companies, who operated what amounted to a closed shop. The Mercers, reflecting the traditional power of the English wool trade, were the most prestigious of all the companies but the Goldsmiths were by far the richest. The livery companies became exemplars of wealthy Londoners' new taste for luxury: they were consumers of gold, silks, furs and expensive imported foodstuffs and their feasts were famous for excess and extravagance.

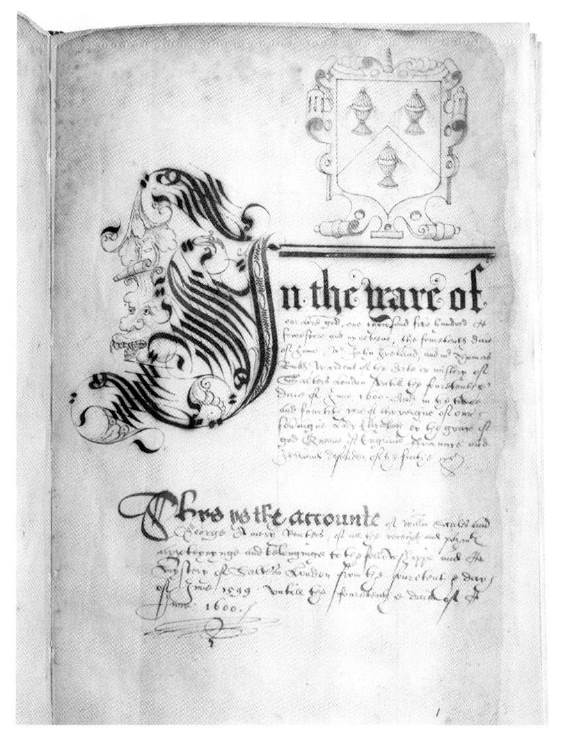

In the yare of

One of the few documents in the Salters' Company archive to have survived the Great Fire, this one, from 1599, shows the Company's coat of arms.

Billingsgate Market, *c.*1598. Billingsgate was one of the Thames-side quays where ships carrying salt, usually from France, would dock.

The Salters had established complete control over the trade in imported salt used in cured fish and meat – a vast enterprise in a time when salting was the most important means of preserving food. According to company regulations, non-members, known as 'foreign', had to apply for licences to practise their trade and anyone found employing a 'foreigner' without a licence was heavily fined.

Though little survives of the Salters' records before 1600, we can infer something of Henry's working experience from the prescribed ways in which men proceeded through company and City life generally. Henry almost certainly entered the company as an apprentice, which in prestigious City companies usually happened in a boy's late teens and generally required a substantial premium to be paid upfront. His master may well have been not only a Salter by company but a salter by trade although – as Henry's own career was to show – it was increasingly becoming the case that company membership and occupation did not necessarily go together.

Being bound apprentice was a necessary step to gaining control over one's own business, trade or craft. It was a hard grind: there was the daily supervision of the master and regular whippings for offences and many were not released until their early 30s. No wonder then that among apprentices there was a steady dropout rate of forty to fifty per cent.

Every step up the ladder of preferment brought increasing privileges. Some apprentices progressed no further than the rank of journeyman, employed by a master craftsman and paid a daily wage; others became 'householders', which meant they owned their own premises. Being a respectable householder, keeping one's nose clean, could lead eventually to the privilege of wearing the fur-trimmed robe and silk hood of the liveryman.

Membership of a livery company therefore had many perks and advantages, though it was expensive too: at the turn of the seventeenth century, the accounts of the Haberdashers' Company show that they would regularly spend £100 on a single dinner

– relying on generous contributions from members. Yet once you had achieved membership of a company, you had access to funds that would help with securing tools or provide the possibility of low-interest or interest-free loans.

They looked after their own. All the companies ran almshouses and took care of deceased members' widows and children. It was considered quite normal for members to use the machinery of the company to distribute some of their wealth by endowing schools or other charitable offices, often supplemented after the member's death by his widow.

Thomas Beamond's almshouses in Bread Street were in 1454 left to the Salters' Company by Beamond to administer (he also left them the property which became Salters' Hall in the same street). Sir Ambrose Nicholas, a wealthy Salter who was Lord Mayor of London in 1575, donated the row of almshouses that were situated in Monkwell Street. Sometimes these bequests made use of other livery companies: the Salter Robert Fleming left several

Liverymen at Queenhithe (sometimes known as Saltwharf). Salt traders were required by law to sell direct to the citizenry on the quayside before they went to the larger curing fisheries. From Hugh Alley, *A caveatt for the citty of London*. Manuscript, 1598.

The Lenard Fireback, 1636, from Lewes in Sussex is made from Wealden iron and depicts an ironmaster and his tools. Wealden iron was the source of Henry's first fortune.

bequests to charity in his will, including £67 to the Fishmongers' Company, the income to be used to help poor people who relied on fish trimmings for food, and a similar amount to the Butchers to help poor people who came to their 'shambles'* for meat refuse. Robert Parkhurst, the overseer of Henry Smith's will, left £20 in his own will of 1636 to the Clothworkers' Company to be distributed amongst the poorer members and their dependants as they thought fit; he also bequeathed £40 to the master, wardens and livery to pay for a dinner on the day of his funeral.[3]

As a member of the Salters who had worked out his apprenticeship, Henry was one of the three out of four male citizens of London who were freemen of the City. Many at this stage went back to their own counties to establish themselves there; others stayed in London and tried to make it in the commercial hurly burly of the city. This seems to have been what Henry Smith chose to do, quietly inching his way into a position of influence.

For a freeman, the next rung up was to become a member of the livery of the company - and 'enclothed'. This meant being entitled to wear the distinctive dress that demonstrated one's company allegiance (the Salters' colours were blue and yellow). There are few surviving records of the Salters before 1599, though Henry is listed in their accounts of that year as being two shillings in arrears with his annual dues. It is possible that he may have risen to membership of the court of assistants, the small group who led the company, and perhaps even became one of its chief officers, perhaps a warden. There are later references to a 'Mr Smith' being Master of the Salters in 1615 but there is no further evidence that this is Henry or even that at this stage he had any interest in the company; his will, for example, makes no mention at all of the Salters. It is possible of course that he overlooked them because he had fallen out with them for some reason – as incidents in his later life demonstrate, he was prone to falling out with his associates – so the mastership of 'Mr Smith' remains an intriguing footnote to what we know of Henry's story.[4]

What we can be more certain of is that during the early 1590s Henry was living in the parish of St Dunstan-in-the-East (between Tower Bridge and the Tower of London). Stow, in his *Survey of London*, described St Dunstan's as 'a great parish of many rich merchants, and other occupiers of diverse trades, namely salters and ironmongers.' There is evidence too that Henry was becoming prosperous during his time living in St Dunstan's parish – a Henry Smith was cessed (assessed for tax) in Tower Ward in 1582 for £10 and in 1589 for £50.

A stray snippet from a later court case gives us the reason: Henry was working in the iron business, trading in the iron produced by the profitable manufacturers of the Weald region of Kent. During the sixteenth and seventeenth centuries this was the most important iron-producing region in England. In 1628, just a few months after Henry's death, Richard

* The Anglo-Saxon word *fleschshammels* were the shelves on which butchers would display their meat and was the origin of the word shambles.

Amherst, who was a trustee of Henry's estate, filed a Complaint against the executors of the will, in which he described in his defence the origins of his friendship with Henry. Amherst had been a law student at Gray's Inn when the two men met, he tells us: 'being when your Orator first knew him Citizen and Salter of London & dwelling at or nigh St Dunstan's Hill in the City of London & then used the trade of buying & selling of iron'. Henry would then have been in his forties. After Amherst was called to the bar in 1592, his professional services were employed by Henry on several occasions in 'much trading businesses' as well 'making of his assurances upon mortgage for loan of money and in some of his purchases of lands and afterwards in letting of his lands receipts of his rents and accounting for the same and paying thereof to his use and ordering of his houses and buildings.'[5] From this we learn that Henry had a substantial property portfolio and was lending money on a large scale.

It was highly likely that Henry during this period would also have served in local government: it has been calculated that in any one year one in ten of London's citizens were serving as parish or City officers. If he acted as a parish officer or a vestryman, Henry would have had to deal with the running of his parish, which in the late sixteenth century would have meant confronting the consequences of poverty – and both its punishment and its relief.

Membership of a livery would have also entitled Henry to stand as a councilman and then to be put up for nomination as an alderman; and this he did. On 9 February 1609, the Lord Mayor reported his nomination to the ward of Farringdon Without, to succeed Henry Vylett, a member of the Fishmongers.

> The inhabitants of the said ward did nominate Sir Stephen Soame, Sir Thomas Bennett, Knights, Wm. Cockayne, Skinner and Henry Smith Salter of which

All that remains of St Olave's Church in Silver Street is this small stone tablet marking the spot where Henry's parish church once stood.

> noiacon [nomination] this court did accept and allow, and thereupon this court preceding to election by scrutiny . . . the said Henry Smith was chosen Alderman of the said Ward and thereupon it is ordered that he shall be warned to make his personal appearance in this Court on Tuesday next to take his oath accordingly.[6]

The swearing-in took place five days later, on 14 February; Henry was 59 years old. He was an alderman for only a few months, however, being recorded as discharged in May the same year. It is likely he regarded it as a prestigious appointment, a display of the full splendour of City citizenship (its status demonstrated by the aldermanic robes he wears on his monument). Full influence would have come with the exercise of office but Henry avoided those responsibilities – perhaps keen not to incur the expenses that went with them. Being an alderman was very costly: aldermen generally required substantial private incomes if they were to afford to subsidise the civic feasting and conviviality demanded by the

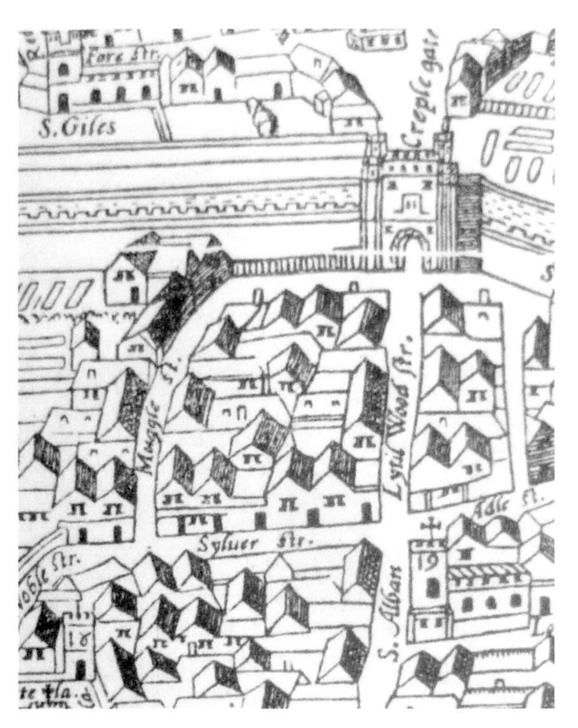

A detail from the Agas Map, *c.*1561, showing Silver Street and its neighbourhood.

livery companies. This meant that the office was generally the preserve of the wealthy.

In 1611, Henry bought himself a substantial house in Silver Street, in the parish of St Olave's. Silver Street was in Cripplegate, close to the London Wall and what is now the Barbican. The church of St Olave's (dismissed in Stow's *Survey* as 'a small thing without any noteworthy monuments') was an early medieval building that was remodelled in 1609, just two years before Henry Smith arrived to take up residence in Silver Street. It was in this house that he was to die and in which he made his will: the site of the house remained in the possession of his charity until Silver Street was finally flattened in a German air raid on 29 December 1940.

Most of the medieval buildings that were once clustered along Silver Street went up in flames in the Great Fire of 1666 and were replaced in the seventeenth century by stone houses and later by Victorian warehouses. A small stone tablet showing a skull and crossbones still survives, set into a section of wall inside a small patch of grass squeezed between the tower blocks that now dominate what was once Silver Street. The words inscribed on it read: 'This was the parish church of St Olave Silver Street, destroyed by the dreadful fire in the year 1666.' The fire also consumed many of the parish records that might, perhaps, have given us some more small clues to Henry Smith's period of residence in the parish.

John Stow says of sixteenth-century Silver Street only that there were 'divers fair houses' along it. He speculates that the street's name came from the number of silversmiths that lived and worked there in medieval times – but by the late sixteenth and early seventeenth centuries, there were no silversmiths left there, though there were a number of goldsmiths. During the years between 1603 and 1612, the burial register of St Olave's lists the dead along with their trades: among them scriveners, embroiderers, salters, tailors, a waver, a cook, a needlemaker and a minstrel; it gives some clue to the rich variety of crafts and occupations which the parish supported. Down a small alleyway between Silver

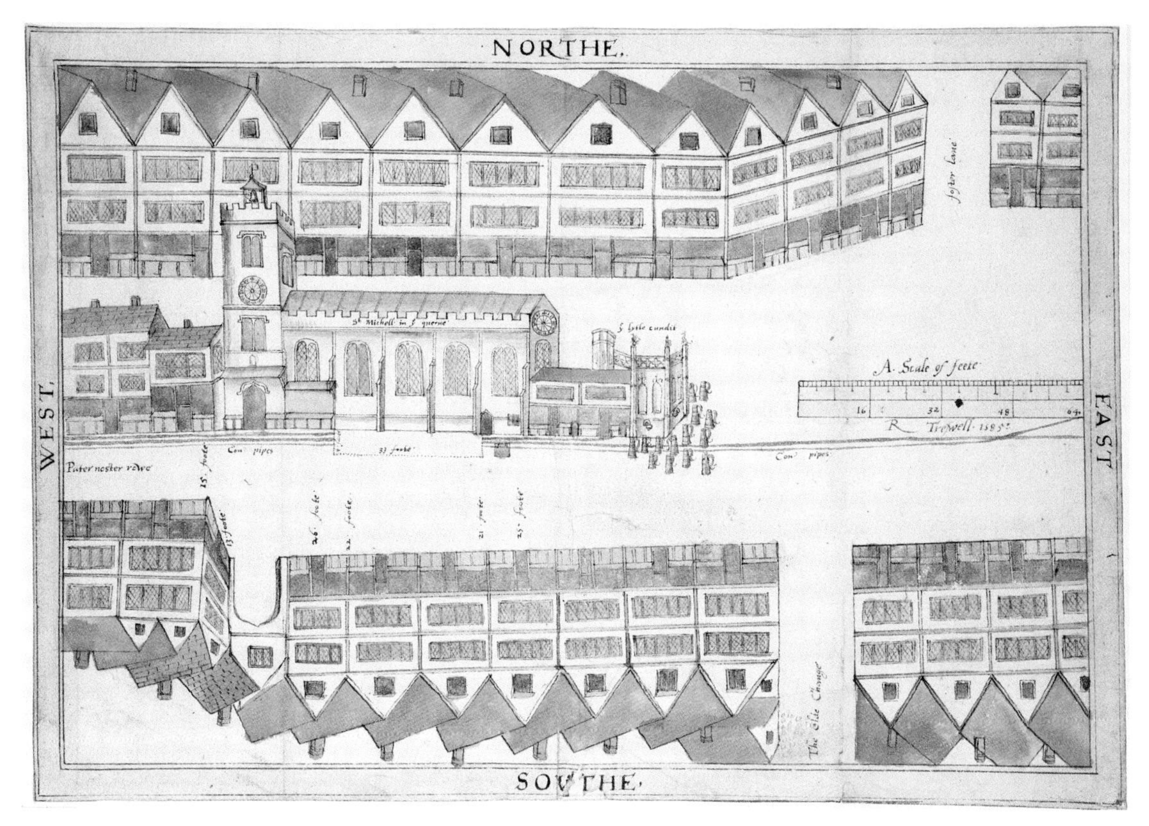

Cheapside in 1585 by Ralph Treswell. This busy commercial thoroughfare ran close by Silver Street. It was at the heart of Henry Smith's London.

Street and Wood Street was a tavern and wine shop called The Talbot – a well-known watering hole for roisterers.

Jacobean Silver Street's most celebrated resident was William Shakespeare: he lodged there for a period between 1602 and 1605 with a Huguenot tire-maker (headdress maker) called Christopher Mountjoy and his wife, Marie, who lived in a house on the east side of the street where it dissects Monkwell Street, right opposite St Olave's. During the period of Shakespeare's residence the parish priest was John Flint, a Cambridge graduate with a reputation as a fiery preacher and puritan. He was still the priest there in 1611, when Henry moved to Silver Street.

Silver Street was at the heart of the City, close to the great commercial thoroughfare of Cheapside and the medieval cathedral of St Paul's. Before the 1666 Fire, the houses there would have been timber-framed tradesmen's dwellings – of the kind that would have been roomy enough to take in lodgers. Henry Smith purchased his house from a Mr Hordson and it was reported to be spacious: it had a frontage of more than 21 feet at the front and extended to 35 feet at the back. That is all that is known of its appearance and dimensions but a 1599 plan of one of the Silver Street houses, Dudley Court, has survived and gives some clue as to how Henry Smith's home might have looked. Dudley Court, once owned by Queen Elizabeth's Sergeant of the Pastry, was set back from the street, with entry via a courtyard; there were three floors and an irregular frontage of about 60 feet; in the main part of the house there were four rooms on the ground floor, including a kitchen and what we might now think of

In this woodcut from a broadsheet ballad Debt stalks ordinary folk.

as a parlour. There were eight upstairs rooms, most of them poky, apart from one large chamber with a fireplace; there was also a 'privy' measuring five feet by seven. Outside the house there was a long, narrow, walled garden with a well in it.

In his will, Henry left his gardener, Augustine Daborne, £10 – which suggests that his house had a garden to be proud of. Silver Street at this time had some fine gardens: one of them belonged to Lord Windsor and another, on the corner of Monkwell Street, belonged to the Barber-Surgeons' Company, who in the 1630s built their famous circular anatomy theatre there. The garden of Barbers' Hall had a hedge of sweet briars and plantings of strawberries, rosemary, violets and vines. Other livery companies also had their headquarters in the neighbourhood of Silver Street, adding to its general reputation for wealthy respectability. Nearby were Bowyers Hall, Curriers Hall, the Plasterers, the Brewers, the wealthy Haberdashers, the Embroiderers, and the Goldsmiths.

About Henry Smith's neighbours in Silver Street there are only fragments surviving – but among the more prominent of them is the celebrated surgeon Master John Giffard, who attended at the bedside of the 20-year-old Henry Prince of Wales as he lay dying in 1612. It is not too far-fetched to speculate that Giffard might also have attended Henry Smith in his last illness, though a Dr Tench is the physician named in Henry's will.

By the time of Henry's move to Silver Street he was in his sixties and the possessor of a substantial fortune. There are clues dating from the 1570s as to his involvement in the controversial practice of moneylending. Debates surrounding lending or borrowing with interest were heated in the late sixteenth century in England. The fluid land market, investment in industries such as coal mining and iron manufacture, the growth of overseas markets – all these were underpinned by moneylending, a practice condemned as usury in the Old Testament. Medieval theologians, in particular Thomas Aquinas, had concluded that lending with a return above the principal was counter both to natural law and the word of God. The debates hinged on whether one took Aquinas's objectivist view of moneylending as an act against the law of nature or whether you took the subjectivist view that it was evil intent alone that made lending with interest a sin.

Details and exceptions were propounded (the Lateran Council of 1215 for example permitted lending at interest to support charitable deeds) but although the practice of moneylending was still morally ambiguous, it was widespread, and many,

Henry Smith among them, took advantage of the new attitudes and looser regulations. It was by this means that Henry acquired, as security for debts, large landholdings. More importantly, he had become a key figure in the lending of money to the aristocracy at a period when many noble families were racked with debts incurred through political turmoil and booming consumerism. His growing web of influential connections proved useful in the furtherance of his career and, later, in the progress of his philanthropic legacy.

Each recorded debt tells us something of how close these transactions brought Henry to the centres of political and court power. An early recorded debt might not involve our Henry Smith, as he would, by 1579 when it was secured, have been only a young man just out of apprenticeship. But the evidence in favour of it being our Henry is that it touches on several later areas of influence in his life. This Henry Smith lent £400 to Lord Mountjoy in order that he might continue to raise mortgages on the alum mines that he owned in Dorset. He received security on the loan of a 12-year lease to manufacture an annual 200 tons of copperas (a sulphate widely used in the dyeing process).[7] The Mountjoy family, however, fell into a disagreement with Henry Hastings, the third Earl of Huntingdon. The mines were on manors and lands owned by Huntingdon and leased to the Mountjoys. On the death of Lady Mountjoy, the title in the mines that her husband had vested in her passed to her sons and Huntingdon sought to assert control over them: this precipitated six years of complicated litigation and mounting debt for all parties.

In this imaginary procession of the Order of the Garter at Windsor by Marcus Gheerhaerts the Elder, 1576, the Earl of Huntingdon is pictured second from the left.

The strongly Protestant Huntingdon was by this time a key figure in the court and government of Queen Elizabeth I. He also, however, had a great number of dependants, in the form of his mother and several siblings, and his long years of royal service had made huge inroads into his extensive private capital. By the time of his death, the Hastings family fortune was all but dissipated. Henry Smith, as seems by now his custom, appears to have been on hand with some much-needed loans. His involvement in the Huntingdon family (and this time we can be sure it is our Henry Smith) is further exposed in an intriguing Chancery suit in 1597, as the tangled consequences of Huntingdon's matchmaking and financial problems brought Henry into dispute with Sir Thomas Posthumous Hoby and his wife, Margaret.[8]

Margaret, whose diary is the earliest known by an Englishwoman to survive, was the daughter of a Yorkshire gentleman, Arthur Dakins. She was brought up a rigorous puritan in the Earl of Huntingdon's household. Furthermore, as her biography in the Oxford DNB notes, 'As an heiress she was a valuable commodity in the Elizabethan marriage market, and she was married three times, to well-connected younger sons approved by the Hastings family.' She married first, in 1588 or 1589, Walter Devereux, younger brother of Elizabeth's favourite, the Earl of Essex, and stepson of the Countess of Huntingdon's brother the Earl of Leicester. Her father and the Devereux brothers bought the manor of Hackness in Yorkshire to settle on the couple. For their share of the purchase price, the Devereux borrowed £4,000: the property itself was security for the loan, conveyed to the creditors upon trust and assurance that upon repayment of the debt it should be conveyed to Walter and Margaret. Matters were thrown into disarray by Walter's premature death at the siege of Rouen in 1591. Within months, Margaret had married another kinsman of the Countess of Huntingdon, her nephew Thomas Sidney. To support the new match, the earl guaranteed that he should redeem Hackness from the creditors and settle it on Margaret and her new husband. This actually meant that the debt was taken over by Sir John Harington, a kinsman of Sidney's, and Edward Mountague: again upon assurance of conveying the estate to the couple upon repayment.

With half the debt still unpaid, Huntingdon then turned to Henry Smith. The manor was conveyed to Henry, and also to Giles Fleming and William Bond, 'citizens of London', who bought out the debt on Huntingdon's behalf. Again, it was planned that it should be settled on Margaret and her husband once the debt was paid. And then, in 1595, whilst the sale of the property was in progress, Thomas Sidney died, and a few months later Huntingdon followed, obtaining Margaret's promise on his deathbed that she should marry Thomas Hoby, which she duly did in August 1596. Henry Smith, according to Hoby, insisted on standing by the sale and holding on to the property even though Sir Thomas had offered to pay off the debt. 'And although the complainant have sundry times offered Henry his money with consideration for the forbearing thereof, and has required the assignment of the premises according to the trust, he still refuses to do so.'

According to Henry, Huntingdon had complained to him that 'he was out of great sums of money for Master Sidney without any means to relieve himself but by Hackness'. The earl had offered Smith £2,000 (with ten per cent interest and the manor as security) to buy out Harington, with the intention that it should eventually be settled on the earl or whomever he chose. Smith had done so, but had not received a penny in repayment nor been able to receive any profits from the manor because he had been kept from the deeds of the estate, and had financially suffered from the deal.[9]

The parties duly came to an agreement confirmed by decree in Chancery on 28 June 1597. Sir Thomas would pay Henry: upon full payment of £3,520, Henry would release all claims to the estate to Sir Thomas and Dame Margaret. Although the Hobys portrayed Henry as inflexible and flouting the true intention that the property was always intended for

A view of the River Severn on Henry Smith's estate at Longney in Gloucestershire. The estate was purchased in 1602 and still belongs to the charity.

The Henry Smith Charity still owns the estate at Warbleton in Sussex which Henry bought in 1615. Warbleton was famous for its iron manufactory and furnaces and this clearing on the estate suggests the site of an old ironworks.

Margaret and whomever she might marry, the whole case has something of the air of collusive action. Both sides agreed on how Huntingdon had turned to Henry to buy out the debt, and what was at stake was resolving the complications caused by the untimely deaths of Margaret's second husband and the earl.

Henry struck a hard bargain, somewhat in excess of the amount due, and he probably benefited from the need of the Hobys to get the matter settled, as they were also facing claims on the property from Huntingdon's brother and successor, who was trying to claim the estate for himself.

Henry appears to have further consolidated his reputation as a fixer for the impoverished aristocracy. Moneylending was not a trade that would ensure him a reputation for virtue: after his death, the Attorney General was to comment darkly 'that there was one Mr Smith in London a man well known what he was'.[10] Nonetheless, in this period we see Henry rapidly accumulating the land and properties, some due to foreclosed mortgages, that were to become the sources of the income of Smith's Charity.

A detail of one of the third Earl of Dorset's shoes – from a 1613 portrait of him by William Larkin. The earl's wild extravagance on luxuries and fashionable clothes ruined his estate.

In 1595, he purchased the manor of Eastbrooke in Southwick, on the coast of East Sussex, from the Earl of Nottingham; in April 1597, Henry loaned Thomas Waller £1,125 on the security of two manors and a few acres of marshland in Kent; in 1602, he is named with Lord Lumley as joint owner of the manor of Longney in Gloucestershire; in 1614, he purchased from the third Earl of Dorset the manor of Notcliffe in Gloucester for £1,500; and a year later, in 1615, he purchased the manor of Warbleton on the slopes of the Weald in West Sussex from ironmaster Sir Thomas Stollion. Sussex was familiar country to Henry, as it was a leading site of the iron industry that had been his trade in the 1590s, and the sale included the Markly Rushlake furnace. In 1622, he became owner of the Somerset estate of Newton St Loe. By the time of his death Henry had in his possession lands in several counties, including Gloucestershire, Essex, Sussex, Somerset, Worcestershire, Middlesex, and Kent.

Through moneylending, Henry was also brought close to families who held political influence – and to their financial ruin. In 1616 and 1620, for example, Robert Devereux, the third Earl of Essex (a connection possibly secured by those earlier dealings with the Earl of Huntingdon, to whom the Devereux family was related) bound himself to repay Smith debts of £103 6s 8d and £525.[11] The earl would later become, like so many of Henry's debtors, a trustee of Smith's Charity.

The heart of Henry's landholding, however, and of his large network of debt and credit in the 1620s, lay in Sussex, where his fortunes were increasingly closely bound to those of the Sackvilles, the family of the Earls of Dorset. Most significant of all, however, was Smith's close involvement in the erratic financial fortunes of Richard Sackville, the third Earl of Dorset, a 'licentious spendthrift', who single-handedly

A portrait by Isaac Oliver of Richard Sackville, third Earl of Dorset, in 1616, eight years before his death. His vast debts threatened the stability of Henry's charity.

dissipated the Sackvilles' millions. As the debts of the third earl soared, Henry also became involved in his financial expedients, eventually buying the Sackvilles' mansion at Knole, in Kent, and leasing it back to the family for £100 per annum.

The third earl was born in Charterhouse, London, in 1589, the son of the second earl and a grandson of the Duke of Norfolk. His marriage in 1609 to the hugely wealthy Lady Anne Clifford, daughter of the Earl of Cumberland, was tumultuous and unhappy – she was cooped up in Dorset's newly refurbished Knole mansion, while her husband, a brazen philanderer, went to court to fight for the inheritance and estates claimed by his wife in Yorkshire. They had five children: three sons who died early and two daughters. The earl's will (which runs to thirty-seven pages) gives an idea of his extravagant tastes – indulgences which were later to leave his estate in financial ruin: they include a 'rock ruby ring' and 'three score silver vessels', six silver candlesticks weighing 128 ounces each and, as an example of his passion for gorgeous costume, his cassock 'lined with green cloth and laced with green and black silk lace'.

The debts Dorset accrued with Henry Smith brought Henry close into the Sackville circle in Sussex – the two men may have first met through Dorset's steward Richard Amherst, an old friend of Henry. The connection cemented Henry's influence in the iron-manufacturing areas of Sussex and Kent, where the Sackvilles had their estates, and from where so many of the earlier trustees were to be drawn.

In the early years of the seventeenth century, Henry was closely involved in the Sackvilles' wider family and household. As we will see, there were links to the family, and through them to many others in Sussex and Kent, in a large number of the original trustees Henry chose for his charity. In 1606 he was a witness to the marriage agreement between Sir Edward Sackville (later fourth Earl of Dorset) and Mary Curzon; and he went on to remember the bride in his will, leaving her £200 to divide between her children. Henry was also appointed a trustee of the Sackville Almshouses in East Grinstead that were established in 1609 with money left by Robert Sackville, second Earl of Dorset.

A number of Henry's transactions involved Sir William Bond, who had been an important player in the case against Sir Thomas and Lady Hoby. In 1608, Bond was named in a survey of men and arms for the militia as Lord of the Manor of Longney, indicating his connections to the expanding empire of Henry Smith's landholdings. Bond was a well-known figure in London commercial and political life, the owner of a large property in Highgate (later Lauderdale House), which had fine gardens and ten acres of pasture. It was here in 1611 that Lady Arbella Stuart, who had until recently been first in succession to the throne, stopped on her way back to London in disgrace after a marriage forbidden by King James I. Pleading illness, Lady Arbella stayed in Highgate with the Bonds for six nights – and the Bishop of Durham, accompanying her, wrote that Sir William and his wife 'had a very especial care both of her and of such as were about her'; she was to die, mad, in the Tower four years later. The government paid Bond's expenses for this episode – and the record lists £7 12s 6d for 'divers persons who took pains at Highgate'.

Bond was a Haberdasher and the nephew of Sir George Bond, who had been Lord Mayor in 1587. He was also a close associate of Henry's cousin Anthony Smith, son of Sir Thomas Smith of Campden; Bond was also distantly related through his aunt to the Throckmortons (and, incidentally, to Robert Catesby the gunpowder plotter). Both men were connected with the influential family of Sir Richard Martin, who twice served as Lord Mayor: Anthony married Martin's daughter Joan and Bond's sister Anne married Joan's brother Richard. At some point just after the death of Anthony Smith in 1611, it was Bond, administering his estate, who brokered the completion of Anthony's sale of the manor of Campden to Baptist Hicks, a wealthy merchant, influential politician – and also a moneylender. Tying the Bond

KNOLE

Knole House, surrounded by a thousand-acre deer park, is almost unchanged in appearance since 1600. When Henry Smith purchased the house from the executors of the third Earl of Dorset, however, the splendid renaissance façade would have been new. The first Sackville owner of Knole, Thomas the first Earl of Dorset (born in 1536), was a second cousin of Anne Boleyn and rose to become a powerful courtier, statesman, diplomat, Chancellor of Oxford University and, finally, Lord Treasurer. Sussex, particularly the area near Lewes, had been the Sackville power base since the twelfth century; their seat there was Buckhurst Park – for generations after they moved to Knole, the Sackvilles continued to be buried in the family chapel at Withyham on the Sussex North Downs.

A detail of the staircase at Knole House, the Sackvilles' seat near Sevenoaks, which came into the possession of Henry Smith and remained with the charity until 1792.

The Sackvilles had amassed vast wealth during the dissolution of the monasteries by buying former monastic land; they prospered further by becoming suppliers of timber for the Wealden iron industries. In 1570, Thomas Sackville, who had accrued new properties all over Kent and Sussex, took a lease on a fine medieval manor house near Sevenoaks called Knole, formerly a seat of the Archbishop of Canterbury, and set about refurbishing it. It was a vast project that took years to complete: thousands of craftsmen worked on remodelling the old house in the Renaissance style, with gables and new mullioned windows, and producing sumptuous panelling, embroidered hangings, furniture and tapestries for the interior. Thomas Sackville did not live to see the work at Knole, but his son, the second earl, was the first Sackville to make Knole his main home; after his death in 1609, Buckhurst Park was demolished (a single tower still stands today) and the stones used to build a hospital at East Grinstead, 'for the relief of 31 unmarried persons'.

family yet tighter to Smith and his world is the fact that Bond's cousin was George Whitmore, who was to become one of the trustees of Smith's Charity. Sir William died in 1617 but Henry Smith was to remember his two daughters in his will.

Another key business associate during Henry Smith's later years (and a trustee in the Deed of 1627) was William Rolfe, a much younger man (he was born in 1594), who appears to have been the chief mediator in Henry's affairs during his final years in Silver Street. The Attorney General in 1626 described him as 'Mr Rolfe the scrivener. A man much trusted and employed by Mr Smyth'[12] and he was an executor of the 1627 will. On 7 May 1620, William Rolfe appears among the signatories on the note of delivery that bound the Earl of Essex, among others (including Rolfe's later business partner, Ralph Massie), in £1,000 owed to Henry Smith. The condition was that Essex or one of his fellow debtors pay £525 to Smith on 8 November 1620 at the dwelling of 'William Rolfe Scrivener, of Fleet Street'. (A scrivener was anyone with professional penmanship skills – an accountant, lawyer, public servant or secretary.) Rolfe's name appears in a number of financial transactions in this period, several of them involving in some capacity trustees or future trustees of Smith's Charity.

Many of Rolfe's property transactions may have related to moneylending. In 1638, by which time he was facing considerable financial difficulties, he and Ralph Massie were fined a total of £1,550 as a result of suits brought, among others, by the Countess of Castlehaven, who had deposited £1,000 with them. Wheeler-dealers, speculators and fixers like Rolfe lived on a knife-edge.

THE LAST YEARS

Henry Smith spent the last years of his life meticulously, even obsessively, planning the disposal of his wealth. Now in his seventies, his wife was dead and he had no surviving children; according to Richard Amherst, 'in his latter age grown weak and infirm in body by a great rupture and being hard of hearing', he was virtually housebound. Richard Lumley, later a trustee, recounted that Henry was already giving money to charity 'with his own hand and others of his appointment.'[13] But his chief remaining interest was the establishment of his philanthropic legacy – though this was to prove more complicated than he had anticipated.

By October 1619, when he was aged 71, Henry had established a series of trusts that marked his first attempt to ensure that following his death, his wealth would be distributed for charity in the manner of his choosing. He prepared a deed under which the bulk of his property was to be conveyed to seven nominees who would then distribute the rental income for charitable purposes (at this point these were not made specific), after allowing Henry £500 a year for his own maintenance in Silver Street.

Most of the nominees he selected for this purpose were connected to the Sackvilles and to Sussex; the exceptions were William Bond's kinsman George Whitmore, William Wingfield and the Earl of Essex. Furthermore, most of them owed him money – and their debts were written into this deed, and appointed to charitable uses. Henry remained in possession of his property and the nominees continued to pay him interest on their debts. Henry laid out the deed – in terms that were, as far as he was concerned, unambiguous – to ensure that the trustees who owed him money were not to be relieved of the responsibilities of repayment. As well as the earls of Essex and Dorset, the trustees at this stage were Wingfield, Whitmore, Edward Francis, John Middleton and Richard Amherst. Although the evidence is contradictory, it seems likely that Sir Richard Lumley was also at this time a trustee. Certainly Lumley, although then only 30 years old, seems to have become a key member of Henry's inner circle – or, as Henry seems by most available accounts to have been a prickly and controlling type, what approximated to an inner circle.

The 1619 deed was clearly precautionary: Henry retained control of his property and also retained the

THE THREE 1626 TRUSTEES

SIR JOHN MIDDLETON

The Middletons owed their prosperity to the Wealden iron trade. John Middleton was born after 1558, in Horsham, Sussex, the only son of an ironmaster. By the 1580s he was a partner in his uncle's gun-founding business – which after 1604 and the peace treaty with Spain, reverted to the iron export trade. As we know that Henry Smith first made his mark as a trader in iron, we can conjecture that the two men met at some time during this period.

Middleton was an important figure in the iron industry, even being cited in 1612 in an official Complaint about the trade's damaging impact on the roads around Horsham. In 1614, he was returned as MP for Horsham – a seat he held for the rest of his life – and in 1624 was created baronet. He was involved in passing a bill for the increase of timber and wood – on which the iron industry was reliant (records show that he and his partners used £4,200 worth of timber from one Sussex park between 1586 and 1589).

Behind Middleton's display of wealth, however, was a mountain of debts – including the £4,000 that by 1620 he owed Henry Smith. Some of these may have been due to his involvement in the finances of the notorious spendthrift Thomas Shelley, whose sister was married to Middleton's son – and he was forced to seek Crown protection from the creditors he had acquired 'by suretyship for Mr. Shelley', assuring the Privy Council that he could, given time, pay off all debts, 'and yet leave a moderate fortune for himself and his children'. He received royal protection while he tried to liquidate his liabilities and early in 1630 he sold the manor of Worth in Sussex to Smith's Charity – although Henry had in 1626 deposed him from his own position as a trustee.

RICHARD AMHERST

Amherst was born in 1565, the son of a yeoman, in Pembury, Kent (fifteen miles from Knole). After Oxford, he trained in Gray's Inn as a lawyer – during which time he first encountered Henry Smith. Amherst was called to the bar in 1592 and by 1606 was practising in Chancery during the period that the first Earl of Dorset was Lord Treasurer. By 1607, Amherst had become a significant figure in the Sackville circle, described in a draft of the first earl's will as 'high steward of all my manors, lands and possessions within the county of Sussex'. He held the post of steward to the Dorset earls for the rest of his life.

Amherst's position and career was closely entwined with the vicissitudes of the Dorset fortunes. In 1609, it was his clergyman brother, Jeffery Amherst, who officiated at the irregular marriage of Richard Sackville and Lady Anne Clifford; and in 1615, Amherst was appointed a trustee for the clearing of the third earl's vast debts. Amherst rented a Sackville house in Lewes and by the 1620s was the highest taxpayer in the town, becoming its Member of Parliament in 1614 and again in 1621. He was appointed a serjeant-at-law in 1623, making him a member of an elite corps of lawyers.

Although he was removed as trustee in 1626, Amherst continued to exercise considerable influence over the future of the charity. As we will see later, he owed Henry £1,000 but refused to repay it to the charity after Henry's death. He died in April 1632, leaving very little estate but bequeathing forty shillings to the poor of the parish of Pembury, 'six weeks boarding and lodging after my decease, they doing their duties and service to my dear wife'.

SIR EDWARD FRANCIS

Born about 1566 in Derbyshire, Francis entered the household of the Earl of Northumberland as steward in 1593. It was this connection that brought him to Sussex, as Northumberland appointed him to run his estate at Petworth. Under the same patronage, Francis secured the Court post of Paymaster of the Gentlemen Pensioners, was returned to Parliament for the seat of Beverley in Yorkshire (1597 and 1601) and of Haslemere in Surrey (1604) and was knighted in 1605. Among his twelve committee appointments was one (somewhat ironically given that he was in hock to Henry Smith for at least £3,000) that considered two bills against usury.

The advancement of Francis' political career was halted suddenly by the involvement of his patron in the Gunpowder Plot of 1605. He continued to run the estate at Petworth while the earl was imprisoned in the Tower but he was removed from the Sussex bench, where he had sat as a justice of the peace. There does not seem to have been any suggestion that Francis was himself involved in the plot but his wife, Elizabeth, was the daughter of a prominent Catholic conspirator, Dr Edward Atslowe, and had herself been prosecuted for recusancy in Sussex in 1605.

Francis continued to have to refute accusations of papism. In 1621, he defended himself against claims by Michael Chambers, a well-known informer, that Lady Francis continued in her popish practices. He protested that he 'cared not a fig (or somewhat worse) for the Pope nor the King of Spain'. Reproved for using undiplomatic language, Francis went on to add 'that he intended it only of the Spaniard's religion, and intended that also no more of him than of all other princes that were of that religion'. He was reported to be 'desperately sick' in 1626, the year he was re-elected to Parliament, and on 23 May he died – and was replaced, by stipulation in the will, as a Smith's trustee by Sir Henry Henn. Francis is buried in St Margaret's, Westminster.

power of revocation of the deed – which was to prove a shrewd move four years later in 1624, when the Earl of Dorset died unexpectedly at the age of 35, leaving confusion and debt in his wake.

Dorset's death, on Easter Day 1624, occurred, according to John Chamberlain, a contemporary writer, after four or five days sickness brought on by 'a surfeit of potatoes'. In his will, Dorset made reference to 'my servant Henry Smith', to whom he bequeathed £10; it seems unlikely that this refers to our Henry, to whom the earl owed a great deal more than that, but it is an intriguing sidelight nonetheless.[14] By the time his debts and legacies of £60,000 had been discharged, he 'left no great matter to his successor' – but he did leave to the executors of his will a large headache, and his tangled finances precipitated a crisis in the arrangements for Smith's Charity.[15]

Dorset's death risked not only the stability of all Henry Smith's legal arrangements with the family but it exposed him to debts of £9,000 owed by those trustees (which was in fact most of them) who had their fortunes linked to the earl, his family or to his influence in Sussex. Henry seems to have been a guarantor for many of Dorset's debts and was therefore left vulnerable – not just regarding his own transactions with the earl but for those of his trustees who were also Dorset's creditors and who

William Larkin's 1618 portrait of Lady Anne Clifford, the celebrated heiress. Her 1609 marriage to the third Earl of Dorset left her incarcerated at Knole while her husband philandered and spent her money.

in turn owed Henry money. Dorset's debts stood at the head of a collapsing line of dominoes – and no one had expected him to die so young.

Faced with a threat to both his estate and his charitable ambitions, Henry was persuaded to accept new deeds that appointed a fresh set of trustees and, more importantly, removed the power of revocation – thus distancing the estate from any future legal claims. Within a few months, and characteristically, he had changed his mind. In a Bill of Complaint in 1624, Henry complained that several of his trustees were now refusing to pay him what they owed – and he also suggested that he was afraid that the call on debts to some of his trustees by other creditors would eat into the Smith property: that their other debts in fact now threatened the wealth and endurance of his estate. It seems that at some point Henry was persuaded by Francis and Middleton 'and others he trusted' to cancel the powers of revocation and convey the entire estate to the trustees, in order to protect it from claims arising from the death of the Earl of Dorset. Henry was later to change his mind, claiming that he had been 'exhorted in a very loving manner' by Francis and Middleton to hand over his estate against his better judgment: by the time he realised what had happened, he wished to have his property reconveyed to him. The trustees, led by Francis and Middleton, refused to comply. Concerned by the instability of his estate, Henry had to resort to the courts to establish that the property was only ever made over to his trustees until he died and that their debts were then to be made over to the charitable causes he had named.

In his testimony to the courts, Henry complained that he had been duped into giving up his right of revocation. But Sir Richard Lumley's response to him provides a different story and demonstrates how insecure a pyramid of debt was represented by the financial positions of the trustees and their associates. Lumley tells us that Edward Lindsey, an executor of the third Earl of Dorset's estate, warned Smith that he was fallen into 'great forfeitures and dangers' from those debts owed to him and for which he had supplied guaranty. Lumley conceded his own debt of £1,000 and stated that Henry had continued to receive the profits of his whole estate (the Lumleys had originally owned the estate at Longney), and Lumley himself had last paid the interest of his debt in the preceding November.

Intriguingly, in a crossed-out passage on this document, Lumley's statement also describes how Henry had privately called Lumley and Amherst (who had drawn up the documents) into his parlour and asked them if, after he had sealed these final absolute deeds, he might afterwards have his estate back again if it fell out that he were clear and free from any danger – to which Amherst had stated that he thought he might.[16]

Henry's deed of 1624 added to the number of trustees the names of Sir George Croke, William Rolfe, Rolfe's uncle Sir William Blake, Sir Christopher Nevill and Sir Richard Gurney. Thus the number now included a highly distinguished judge (Croke), a shrewd man of business (Rolfe) and another influential City man (Gurney). To these trustees and their heirs, he assigned the task of using the rents and profits from his properties to be used in the following ways: for the relief of poor prisoners; 'for hurt and maimed soldiers'; 'poor maids' marriages'; 'setting-up poor apprentices'; 'amending the highways'; and 'losses by fire or shipwreck'.

Although the sums involved were to be on a considerably more munificent scale than most charitable bequests of the time, Henry Smith's concerns were not at the time unconventional. The Charitable Uses Act of 1601 had sought to codify charitable giving in the years after the dissolution of the monasteries by establishing a framework of legally recognised charities. The list of charitable causes drawn up by the Act demonstrates that Henry was in fact operating within clearly defined conventions. According to the Act, a benevolent testator might consider leaving money for 'the relief of aged, impotent and poor people; the maintenance of sick and maimed soldiers and mariners . . . the repair of . . . churches, sea banks and highways . . . education and preferment of orphans . . . and marriages of poor maids'.

On 25 June 1625, the Lord Keeper, Thomas Coventry, decreed that the trustees should be specifically absolved of the charge of misappropriation, that the estate and interest should be vested in the trustees and that Henry himself should retain his house in Silver Street for his lifetime, being free to dispose of the rents and profits of his estate in any manner he thought fit. All those trustees indebted to the plaintiff, Coventry said, should pay their debts before the feast of St Bartholomew the Apostle (24 August). The Lord Keeper also ruled that from henceforth, whenever the number of trustees should fall below six, then the Archbishop of Canterbury, with either the Lord Keeper of the Great Seal or the Lord Chancellor, should intervene to nominate new trustees who would make up the number to thirteen.

Shortly after the Lord Keeper's decree, in 1626, Henry executed a new deed of uses, in which he required his trustees to apply for a royal licence to be granted to the governors of Christ's Hospital – to enable them to take all the Smith lands and manors in perpetuity.* At this point, Henry sacked all those trustees who owed him money – except Sir Richard Lumley. It seems that Henry had also lost faith in the existing arrangements, believing that the administration of his charity should be secured more tightly: an existing charitable foundation such as Christ's had well-regarded systems already established that would collect his revenues and see to their proper distribution. Furthermore, a number of his trustees had associations with the Hospital.

Christ's Hospital, however, refused to accept the trust – for reasons unclear. Henry therefore set about compiling a detailed list of exactly how he wished his charity to be run, how its beneficiaries would be selected and how its overseers at all levels would comport themselves. There were even to be punishments written into the contract to make sure that all involved obeyed the rules. For the first time, Henry planned out how the charity was to fund parishes that would receive annual payments from the profits of assigned estates and how local trustees would be appointed to administer the payments according to the criteria he laid down. The choice of parishes he would leave to his trustees to work out after his death but the principle was here enshrined for the first time.

In these last two years of his life Henry also began to look at other ways to distribute his money – in the form of gifts. In January 1627, perhaps thinking of the county of his birth, he gave £1,000 apiece to the Surrey towns of Croydon, Dorking, Farnham and Guildford; he had already given the same amount to Kingston upon Thames in 1624. In his will, he added Richmond and Reigate to this list; he also bequeathed £500 to Wandsworth.

William Rolfe seems to have been a fairly constant presence in Silver Street. Although Rolfe was then a young man, fifty years Henry's junior, he was added to the final list of trustees, along with Henry Henn, also about the same age, and Henry's nephew Henry Jackson. Rolfe had strong leanings towards the Puritans and was connected with the controversial Feoffees of Impropriations, whose agenda was to procure funds in order to further the nomination of puritan clergy in parishes throughout England. As we will see, Henry's will was to reflect this influence and five years after Henry's death, the Attorney General in 1633 (the year that the Feoffees were officially disbanded) was to cite the fact that Rolfe had persuaded him on his deathbed to leave them money as evidence of the Feoffees' willingness 'to procure money by any means though unfit . . . using a Scrivener to get money from an Usurer'.[17]

Henry's last months at Silver Street were spent working out the final version of his will, the 'making and declaring' of which was finally completed on 28 September 1627. He rarely 'went abroad' during the last decade of his life, according to Richard Amherst, because he had been in poor health. Amherst went on to describe how Henry had been unable to attend services at St Olave's in this period and 'was unjustly presented, indicted & convicted for a popish Recusant'. The recusancy laws at this time were strict: fines were imposed for non-attendance at church and sometimes property was confiscated. Henry was fined £20 for every month of his 'not repairing to church'. According to Amherst's account, Henry pleaded not guilty and Amherst, his lawyer, intervened on his behalf, pleading his friend's infirmity. The case was dropped.[18]

Henry died at the age of 78 on 3 January 1628 and was buried in Wandsworth parish church five weeks later, on 7 February, where the parish register's entry for his burial reads 'Henry Smith, of London, gent'. A funeral certificate in the College of Arms records that

* Christ's Hospital was founded by Edward VI, assisted by the Bishop of London, Nicholas Ridley, and the Lord Mayor, Sir Richard Dobbs, as a response to the dissolution of the monasteries and the resultant increase in the poor and destitute. Via a committee of thirty merchants, Edward donated land in London for the creation of three royal hospitals – Christ's, situated in Newgate, was to be concerned with the education of poor children and it opened its doors in 1552.

Henry wished to be buried at Wandsworth because it was the parish of his nativity. There may have been other reasons that Henry chose Wandsworth, a village that as far as we know he never lived in during his adult life. Walter Smith's public debts and financial ineptitude would have been a source of shame to him: returning posthumously to Wandsworth in some pomp as a prosperous philanthropist would have helped restore the reputation of the Smith family in their original parish.

His funeral was attended by two heralds: Samson Lennard, Blewmantle, deputising for Sir Richard St George, Knight Clarenceaux; and Thomas Thomson, Rouge Dragon. A stone floor slab was laid in the church as his first memorial (though the coffin must have been interred elsewhere: in 1831, the stone was taken up by the churchwardens in Charles Gwilt's presence and nothing was found lying beneath it). On the slab is this inscription:

Depositum Henrici Smith
Senatoris Londinensis
Mole sub hac quaeris quis conditur, optime lector
Cuias et qualis, quantus in orbe fuit
A dextris muri, statuam tu cernere possis
Oranti similem, marmore de Pario;
Subter quam statuam cernatur tabula sculpta,
Auratis verbis quae tibi cuncta notant.

You are interested in the mortal remains of Henry Smith, Alderman of London, who is buried under this slab, [and] dear reader, you can see his lifelike statue in prayer, made of Parian marble, on the wall to the right and [understand] what kind of man he was and how great [he was] in [his] world; underneath which statue can be discovered a tablet engraved with words in gold which tell you everything [about him].

This brass plate can be seen in the floor of Wandsworth church. The original stone slab now lies under a piano and can no longer be deciphered.

Henry Smith's memorial in All Saints Church, Wandsworth, erected after his death in 1628. Dressed in his alderman's robes, he holds a skull, the traditional memento mori of the time.

3

The Will

Henry's will[19] was witnessed by Thomas Costerdine, a Vintner (whose brother was bound apprentice to a member of the Jackson family), Edward Brightwen, Francis Billinge and John Honeybourne. The executors were Sir George Whitmore, George Lowe, William Rolfe, Sir William Blake, Sir Richard Gurney and Henry Jackson. Sir Christopher Nevill, Sir George Croke, Sir Robert Parkhurst and George Duncomb were overseers (appointed by the testator to supervise and assist the executors).

From his personal estate, Henry made a number of personal bequests. These included a fellowship in Cambridge for 'Mr Costerdine's son' in 'some college there to be continued for eight years'. When that fellowship ran its course, the money was to return to Henry Jackson and thereafter was to be used for any of his descendants who might be found 'capable of the place or fellowship from time to time'.* To Henry Jackson himself he bequeathed £1,000.

The Sackvilles, despite the financial chaos unleashed by the third earl, were remembered in the will: Mary Curzon, the wife of the fourth earl, received a bequest of £200 on behalf of her children, and the Countess de la Warr, the widow of a Sackville cousin in Sussex, also received a sum. Other beneficiaries included the two daughters of Sir William Bond, Winifred and Elizabeth, who received £15 each; and Sir Robert and Lady Phelips and their children, who also received £100 pounds. Sir Robert Phelips was born and lived at Montacute House in Somerset, one of the loveliest of English renaissance buildings. The son of Sir Thomas, a Master of the Rolls, Phelips was a celebrated and principled Parliamentarian, and a successful campaigner against monopolies and ministerial corruption and for legal reform. He was also widely acclaimed for his skills in oratory. A fellow Member of Parliament described his delivery rhapsodically: 'A choice store he had and elegance of words, readiness and dexterity in fancy and conception, a voice and pronunciation of much sweetness.' There is no record as to how Phelips and his wife, Bridget, came to be acquainted with Henry Smith – but Joseph Gwilt, the nineteenth-century antiquarian (and father of Charles) found a distant family connection between the Phelipses and the

* The money appears to have run out after the first fellowship and is not referred to again except in 1831 by Charles Gwilt (not only treasurer of Smith's Charity but also kindred), who wrote: 'It would be very satisfactory to know what became of the money; for a fellowship has never been founded, and there have certainly been those of his kindred to whom it would have been of great service, and who were fully qualified for the situation.' (*Notices*, p.47)

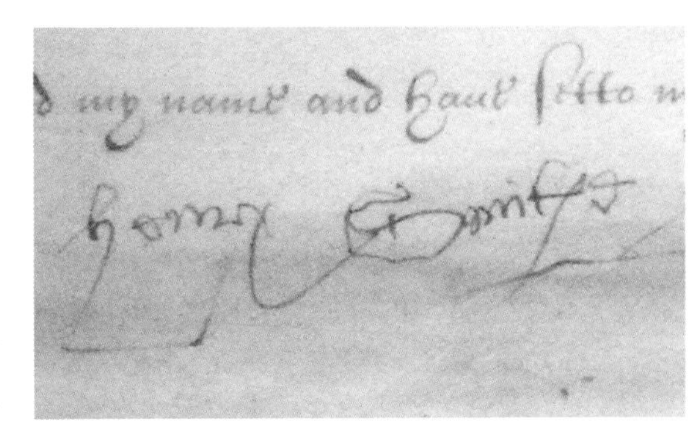

Henry's quavery signature on his will. By this time he was 79 years old and housebound with a rupture.

Despite the chaos unleashed by the third Earl of Dorset's debts, Henry Smith remained close to the Sackvilles. He bequeathed £200 to the children of Mary Curzon (pictured here), the wife of the fourth earl. Portrait by William Hamilton after one by William Larkin, 1645.

Campden Smiths.[20] They may have been introduced to Henry by George Croke, who was among the first trustees of the charity and was, like Phelips, a vociferous opponent in Parliament of ship money. It is highly likely that Phelips was, or had been, another who owed Henry money, as it is known that he was by his own admission 'expensive to the prejudice of our family', and in 1632 was obliged to settle all his estates on his son Edward in order to clear his debts.

Then there was Mrs Price, 'sometime a teacher of children and my kinswoman', who was to have ten pounds; 'Mr. Doctor Lloyd a mourning gown and ten pounds in money'; a mourning gown and ten pounds also went to John Tench, his 'chirugeon' (surgeon); and 'good wife Seabright' and Mr Paytie received fifteen shillings each. Augustine Daborne, the gardener at the house in Silver Street, was left ten pounds. Henry bequeathed to his personal servants

Michael Montgomery and Mary Vavasour ten pounds apiece – although the will stipulated that Michael's portion should skip a generation: 'the said ten pounds to the said Michael should not come into his hands but should be preserved and kept for his the said Michael's child.' The poor of the parish of St Olave's received five pounds in the will and those of St Dunstan's in the East received another five pounds.

'SETTINGE THE PORE ON WORKE'

As well as adding Reigate and Richmond to the five Surrey towns to which he had given £1,000, Henry bequeathed £500 to Wandsworth. When it came to these bequests, Henry makes clear in his will that he drew explicitly on the example of Dorchester, the county town of Dorset, where a radical new project of moral and social reformation had been instigated in the early seventeenth century. The will states that the Surrey towns should look to Dorchester for inspiration in the uses they might make of their £1,000 gift: '[for] the setting of the pore on work and for binding them apprentices and for the teaching and education of poor children as is now used or begun in the Towne of Dorchester'.

Smith had no apparent connections to Dorchester yet this market town with a population of 2,000 had come to represent by the late 1620s an ideal model of Puritan spiritual and civic values; it was seen as a Reformed, godly community, where private philanthropy, combined with efficient urban planning, had achieved a successful level of both social order and charitable relief.

Of the five towns, Kingston was the earliest to receive a gift and was also the earliest to implement it. The manor of Esher Waterville was purchased by the corporation of Kingston in 1628, and the profits were, according to the will, employed explicitly in 'the maintenance and setting on work of the poor of the said Town of Kingston and for the education and bringing up poor people there in some good and Christian course and trade of life'.[21]

'GODLY PREACHERS'

It is probable that Henry Smith learned of John White's work in Dorchester through William Rolfe and Rolfe's associates in the Feoffees of Impropriations. In the will, Henry left £10,000 (to be met by the repayment of 'several debts and sums of money due and owing unto me by Sir Edward Francis, Sir Richard Lumley and John Middleton') for the explicit purchase of 'impropriations' (tithes) that had fallen into lay hands. The income from these would then be used for 'the relief and maintenance of godly preachers and the better furtherance of knowledge and Religion'.

The money for the godly preachers was intended to subsidise preaching of the Word – not parochial livings – at a time when the Laudian church hierarchy was increasingly unsympathetic to both Puritanism and preaching. There is little record of what happened to the fund for godly preachers: it may be that after the Restoration, the triumph of Anglican orthodoxy left no place for the intentions of a previous generation and the fund was then merged into the one created for the relief of poor clergy.

Part of the problem may have been extracting the sums owed by Francis, Lumley and Middleton. From the money that was repaid – only a part of the whole sum – Dorchester received its £300. At the suggestion of the Feoffees of Impropriations, John White started to fundraise in order to purchase property, the income of which was to go to supporting clergy of a Puritan persuasion. White raised £1,500, of which Henry's £300 was a handsome portion – it was eventually put towards the purchase of the parsonage at Seaton and Beer, just over the border from Dorchester in Devon.

'POORE CAPTIVES'

The will also included two bequests of £1,000 to be spent on property that would bring in revenues of at least £60 per annum: these were to be used for the relief of his poor kin and 'for the use of the poor Captives being slaves under the Turkish pirates'.

DORCHESTER

The catalyst that led to Dorchester's transformation was a terrible fire, a 'fire from heaven', that almost completely destroyed the town in 1613. In the aftermath of the devastation it was the fiery Puritan preacher John White, the rector of the parish church of Holy Trinity, who led rebuilding of the town: his intention being to make Dorchester a 'city on a hill', a New Jerusalem. Inspired by White's zeal and oratory, there was a widespread conversion to Puritanism among the inhabitants of Dorchester. A once stagnant provincial town afflicted by unemployment, poverty, disorder and vagrancy thus acquired a reputation as the most 'Puritan' place in England, a beacon of the Reformation.

John White, the fiery and inspirational Calvinist rector of Holy Trinity Church in Dorchester. Woodcut.

John White reorganised Dorchester along radical new lines. A 'Hospital' was established for the 'setting of poor children to work', its aim to eradicate the problem of the moral disorder of idleness among the young. Fifty children were housed there and instructed in 'some lawful trade, mystery or manual occupation' which would enable them to earn a living; furthermore, a Free School was founded, which improved educational opportunities. The sick and elderly were also taken care of with the opening of three new rows of almshouses. This programme of building and charity was funded by a doubling of parish rates and by private charitable giving (including large sums donated at church service collections). But the most lucrative source of funding was the establishment of a municipal brewery, known as the brew-house, which provided not only employment but also income for the building and maintenance of Dorchester's public works and institutions.

The records show that the parish distributed food, clothing, winter fuel and money; they paid paupers' funerals and looked after orphans. In return for relief and security, an increasing amount of control was exercised by John White and the Puritan guardians of the town over the citizens' behaviour: licentiousness, swearing, blasphemy and moral disorder were punished by fining, stocking or flogging.

In 1860, the antiquary Thomas Crofton Croker, in his history of Kensington, claimed that Henry Smith's bequest for the redemption of captives reflected Smith's own experience: 'We know little of the history of this benevolent and extraordinary man, said to have himself suffered a long captivity in Algiers,' he wrote.

While it is true that much of Henry Smith's life is well hidden, one thing of which we can be absolutely certain is that he had no first-hand experience of being held in slavery by pirates. The redemption of captives held by Barbary pirates, however, was not an unfamiliar charitable cause in seventeenth-century Britain and in fact this aspect of his legacy is more conventional than it might now appear.

Since the middle of the sixteenth century there had been a thriving trade in sailors held to ransom by Ottoman or North African corsairs (like European privateers, corsairs were officially legitimised by their governments to raise money for the national coffers). Many of these prisoners were held in captivity for the rest of their lives and of those few who managed to return home, their stories fed the public appetite for terrifying accounts of white slavery and the barbarous 'Musselman'.

Between 1600 and 1640, 800 trading vessels from the British Isles were captured in the Mediterranean and Atlantic and an estimated 12,000 men were captured. Between 1660 and 1730, another 6,000 were sold into slavery. A Catholic priest in 1634 reported that there were 25,000 Christian captives in Algiers and 8,000 of them had become Muslims. Many were housed in *bagnios* (slave prisons) and others worked as agricultural slaves under a sweltering sun, or as galley slaves in the corsairs' long ships. Many survived by converting to Islam – at risk of damnation and of denunciation if they returned home. In 1637, a Laudian rite for 'returned renegades' was devised to accommodate the problem of forcible conversion: 'A form of Penance and Reconciliation of a Renegado or Apostate from the Christian Religion to Turkism,' it involved the former captive being publicly denounced then immediately after that publicly absolved.

Catholic religious orders (particularly the Redemptorists, the Mercedarians and the Trinitarians) were the most celebrated rescuers of Christian captives – travelling in pomp to North Africa bearing papal banners in order to hand over the ransom money; they then took the prisoners home in white garments to symbolise their being washed clean of the taint of their captivity. Since the Reformation, however, English prisoners had few champions in the Catholic orders – and the English state was markedly reluctant to stump up ransom money. As late as 1716, a captive scrawled in a note to his wife: 'All nations is provided for but the poor English has no assistance from their nation.'

By the beginning of the seventeenth century, however, the committee appointed by the Privy Council oversaw campaigns to raise funds for the redemption of captives. The Church of England mobilised support through church collections that accumulated to many millions in today's money, with individual benefactors contributing large sums. Two years before Henry wrote his will, for example, Sir

A seventeenth-century engraving of the slave market in Algiers, where captured sailors were sold into slavery.

ROBERT ADAMS

On 4 November 1625, the father of Robert Adams, a sea captain, was handed a letter with a pathetic message from his son scrawled on the back: 'I pray you pay the post – from a poor captive in Salley.' Salé, then a pirate haven in north-western Morocco, was a prison notorious for the number of captives held there. Robert wrote of his ship being taken by pirates and his subsequent imprisonment:

> For after I was sold, my patron [slave master] made me work at a mill like a horse, from morning until night, with chains upon my legs, of 36 pounds weight apiece, my meal nothing but a little coarse bread and water, my lodging in a dungeon underground, where some 150 or 200 of us lay altogether, having no comfort of the light but a little hole, and being so full of vermin for want of shift [clean clothing] and not being allowed time for to pick myself than I am almost eaten up with them and every day beaten to make me either turn Turk or come to my ransom.

Captain Adams told his father that he had six months to pay a ransom of 370 Barbary ducats. Furthermore, he reported that there were at least 1500 other Englishmen enslaved in Salé but that those who were expected to pay ransoms were used particularly badly.

James Cambel, an alderman, left £1,000 for the captives' cause. They were one of the first examples of disaster appeals, and 'charity briefs', complete with lurid captivity narratives, were used to whip up a horrific picture of the torments and temptations that lay in wait for those held in 'white slavery' under the infidel yoke.

'POOR KIN'

'I give and devise for the use and relief of the poorest of my kindred, such as are not able to work for their living, viz sick aged and impotent persons, and such as cannot maintain their own charge [i.e. of children], the sum of one thousand pounds.' So Henry declared in his will.

As to what prompted the rich and successful Henry Smith to think into the future and make provision for his sister's descendants in perpetuity we can only hazard a guess. Henry knew something of how quickly a family's prosperity can rise and fall, how fortunes can turn on a sixpence.

The 1568 lawsuit between his widowed mother and his father's creditor Kinge suggests that he had experience of the embarrassment of unpaid debts: this case may also have taught him a lesson in the dangers of penury that could be precipitated by the sudden death of the head of the household. In 1627, his thoughts may have been spurred by the recent death of his sister, Joan Jackson, buried in the chancel of Whitechapel parish church on 8 August 1625. Joan was, of course, an old woman at her death but she died in the midst of one of the worst plague outbreaks to hit London in the seventeenth century – Whitechapel saw 53 others go to their graves on that same day. If Joan had died of the plague, it would surely have been to Henry a further sign of the insecurity of life.

Joan had married well, to Henry Jackson, a member of the Grocers' Company, and the Jacksons were in the 1620s comfortably off. We get a glimpse of Joan only through the will of her son Thomas, 'citizen and Haberdasher', a prosperous man, who died in 1629, four years after his mother:

> First and especially I commend and commit my soul into the hands of Almighty God, Father, Son & holy Ghost, assuredly believing through the only merits of the second person of the Trinity Jesus Christ to be saved. My body I commend to the earth to be decently buried in the night time with as small charge and outward Pomp as conveniently may be within the Church yard of the parish of St Marie Matfellon alias Whitechapel in the County of Middlesex at the end of

> the Chancel thereof so near unto the place where my late mother Joan Jackson Widow deceased was buried in the year of our Lord, One thousand six hundred twenty five, as conveniently may bee.[22]

Thomas divided his estate, after the payment of debts and funeral expenses, thus: one third went to his wife, Anne, and one third was to be equally divided among their children: Thomas, Stephen, Sarah, Henry, Mary, Elizabeth, George and Rebecca. They were to be given their portion when they reached the age of 21 (or, for the daughters, if they were married before that age). The final third was to be disposed of in individual payments and any remaining to be shared between his children. His 'dearly beloved and much respected' brother Henry Jackson, for example, received £10 to buy a 'piece of plate in remembrance'. His sister Elizabeth Davis received £5; the children of his late sister Mary Ward and his living sister, Elizabeth Davis, each received forty shillings, as did four named friends who were overseers of the will. His son Thomas was to be given £50 on reaching the age of 21.

The Jackson, Davis and Ward families are the primary source of the pedigrees of Henry Smith's poor kindred. The memorandum of the 1627 will states that Henry Smith was asked by his trustees to make specific his definitions of what he 'meant and intended in and by those words the poorest of this kindred'. His answer was only (and presumably somewhat frustratingly to the trustees, who must have anticipated problems with refining this definition) that 'his meaning was thereby the poorest of his sisters' children and their children successively'.

When Henry talks of his poor kin, he uses a language – 'of poverty, distress or want' – that would more commonly have been used to describe the indigent – yet there is no evidence that the Jacksons or their immediate descendants were anything but prosperous. We know from Thomas's will that his children were all under the age of 21 when he wrote it in 1629: one of his daughters, Rebecca, was married and living in Barbados by October 1650. Henry would surely have been keenly aware, given the experiences of his own youth and the death of his father before he was 21, of the vicissitudes of fortune.

THE DESERVING POOR

From the sums not otherwise disposed of, Henry Smith left in trust to his trustees and executors the revenues accrued from his 'manors, lands, tenements, hereditaments, leases for years extents, rents, charges and annuities to me due or to be due' to be distributed to parishes for the relief of the poor. These properties included the house in Silver Street. The task of selecting which parishes would receive money was left to the trustees.

In his Decree, Henry was prescriptive in his rules on who should receive relief, drawing up criteria that exemplified conventional understandings of need and worth. Recipients were to be the aged and infirm poor, 'married persons having more children born in lawful wedlock than their labours can maintain', orphans, and 'such poor people as keep themselves and families to labour and put forth their children apprentices at the ages of fifteen'. Those excluded from the charity were any given to 'excessive drinking, whoremongers, common swearers, pilferers, or otherwise notoriously scandalous'. The disobedient and the unsettled were also excluded, including vagrants and those who had not lived in the parish for five years. The aged and impotent poor were to receive clothing – 'apparel of one colour, with some badge or other mark, that the same may be known to be the gift of the said Henry Smith'. Alternatively there should be a public distribution of food – so that the onlookers could bear witness to the act of charity it constituted: 'Bread and flesh and fish, upon each Sabbath day publicly in the parish churches of each of the said parishes.'

Henry also thought through the administration of his largesse carefully, setting down guidelines and rules for the parish overseers.

> The church-wardens of each of the said parishes shall, during the time they shall continue in the said offices and places once in every month at the least upon the

LORD HAVE MERCY UPON US.
umble Petition of England unto Alm ghty God, meekely imploring his Divine bounty
Mortality of Peftilence now raigning amongft us : VVith a lamentable Lift of Deaths
in the weekly Burials of the City of LONDON, and the Parifhes adjacent to the fame.

'Lord Have Mercy Upon Us.' A woodcut of 1635 showing the horrors of a mid seventeenth-century plague outbreak in London.

> Sabbath day after evening prayer meet in the church of the said parish to consider of the estate of the poor of the said parish which of them have most need of relief and shall also between the feasts of Easter and Whitsuntide next after the end of every year wherein the said church-wardens and overseers of the poor of that parish . . . upon notice and warning thereof given openly in that parish church immediately after the end of morning prayer make a true and perfect account in a book to be fairly written and kept for that purpose of all their receipts and disbursements for and during the year.

There was also to be a statutory period of fourteen days during which the parish congregation could 'read and peruse' the book and make suggestions or raise objections as to the candidates presented for charitable relief. Any flouting of the rules brought to the notice of the trustees meant a parish forwent its benefit for a year.

The bossily bureaucratic tone of Henry's instructions was not unusual: in fact it echoes the complicated regulations about outside accountability to be found in the 1598 Poor Law Act. That year had seen the final codification of the system of parishes paying poor relief to be funded by money raised through parish rates. Monitored by local magistrates, it not only offered legal security for charities but put into practice a Protestant definition of charity.

Henry Smith, in common with other private philanthropists, would by the 1620s have seen charitable donations as supplements to the provisions provided under the poor law (in fact in his negotiations with Kingston, when the town received his gift of £1,000, he expressly stipulated that his donation was not to interfere with the levying of a poor rate). The poor laws were already the implementation of a highly successful state-sanctioned system of poor relief. Since the early sixteenth century, the economy of England had expanded but not as fast as the population – which had roughly doubled. Wages had fallen and increasing numbers of landless poor, travellers and vagrants could not find work, settlement or housing. They fell too outside the perimeters of poor relief, and hard-pressed parish officers put up barricades against families trying to settle who might in time become a burden on parish funds.

Henry's apportionment for help with the funding of apprenticeships is an attempt to address the problem of family poverty moving from generation to generation. Apprenticeship, for example, or 'binding out' was seen as shifting children from poor families to other, better-off families who would maintain them and set them up in a trade. A rapid increase in legislation to curb and criminalise vagrancy, begging and the refusal to work was coupled with an increasing anxiety as to whether the giving of alms actually stopped people trying to work. The deserving and undeserving poor became roughly categorised as the 'settled' poor and the 'vagrant' poor: and they received different treatment from the authorities.

The first effective legislation to address the problem of poor relief was passed in 1552, within a few years of the destruction of the monasteries and the traditional charitable network that went with them. The idea of deserving and undeserving recipients of charity, of making distinctions between the working poor and the non-working, was rooted in the social order that the legislation was designed to promote. And private philanthropy followed suit: Ambrose Nicholas, for example, the Salter who left a bequest for almshouses in Monkwell Street a half-century before Smith's bequest, stipulated that the residents of his houses should be free of the City (in other words had shown their ability to work) and never to have resorted to begging.

Furthermore, like the recipients of Henry's largesse they were to demonstrate their supplicant status in their dress and behaviour. Nicholas stipulated that his almsmen should wear plain, puritan dress with no ruffs and that 'no householder of the fellowship shall wear any edge of gold or silver, nor of any other colour silk upon their shirts.' Swearing was particularly frowned on and Bartholomew Banks was expelled from the Beamond almshouses for using profane language.

The idea that charitable relief would be dependent on good behaviour was not a new idea in itself – it stems directly from St Paul's 'he who does not work neither shall he eat' – but after the seventeenth century, it deepened in intensity: social order and charity became two sides of the same coin.

A woodcut of *c.*1567, showing a beggar being tied and whipped through the streets. Vagrancy was seen as a symptom of social chaos – and charitable institutions increasingly seen as a tool of moral reform.

4

The First Trustees

THE EARL OF ESSEX
(trustee from 1619)

Robert Devereux, third Earl of Essex, was born in 1591 in Hart Street, London, into a family at the epicentre of Elizabethan political life. His charismatic father was Queen Elizabeth's favourite until political misjudgement sent him to the block; his mother was the daughter of Sir Francis Walsingham, Elizabeth's spymaster-in-chief. When the second earl was executed for treason in 1601, his wife decamped to Ireland with her new husband, and their son, a pupil at Eton, was left virtually penniless. The restoration of his family's good name was to be a driving force of Essex's life. At the succession of James I, Essex, aged 14, was restored of his lands and titles and in 1606 the ambitious Howard family, the earls of Suffolk and Nottingham, arranged his marriage to their daughter Frances. Yet, despite these early indications of favour, the third earl did not prosper in the court of James I: thin-skinned and insecure, Essex was beleaguered by debts that were exacerbated by a taste for gambling and a talent for picking expensive quarrels.

His marriage proved a disaster and in 1613 he was publicly humiliated when his wife's family, the Howards, filed for annulment alleging his impotence. When the court found in their favour, Essex was ordered to repay the Howards their dowry. It is hardly surprising that during this period he had turned to Henry Smith to help him out with loans of money. After incurring the royal wrath for criticising the king in 1614 for

Robert Devereux, the Earl of Essex aged 14, hunting with Henry, Prince of Wales, by Robert Peake the Elder, *c.*1605.

impositions, Essex retreated to his Staffordshire estate for five years, only returning to London to see his former wife and her new husband convicted of poisoning Sir Thomas Overbury. Between 1620 and 1624, Essex served in Protestant armies in the Rhineland and then in the Netherlands. In 1625, he was appointed to lead a British armada to Cadiz, the scene of his father's triumph in 1596. The attempted attack was a disaster, leaving Essex to return home yet again defeated and humiliated. By 1640, having acted for Charles I in the imposition of his Scottish policies, he had returned to London, where he lived in the Strand. He was prominent in the Long Parliament, where he was seen to carry moral and political authority – but then felt himself again overlooked by the king in terms of office. By 1642, he was Lord General – commander-in-chief – of the Parliamentarian forces. Though a Puritan by instinct, Essex was forced from office by the Self-Denying Ordinance of 1645 (by which the Parliamentarian army leaders, many of them aristocrats who favoured peace with the king, were forced to resign their commissions). He was voted £10,000 a year from confiscated Royalist lands but he was gradually eclipsed from public life. In 1646, after a day's stag-hunting in Windsor Forest, Essex had a stroke – and died four days later. He was accorded a magnificent state funeral on 26 October 1646 attended by 3,000 – yet his fine tomb in Westminster Abbey was destroyed at the Restoration.

SIR GEORGE WHITMORE
(trustee from 1619 and executor of the will)

Born in London about 1572, the financier Sir George Whitmore was a Royalist sympathiser. An august figure in the commercial world of Jacobean London, Whitmore came from a family with distinguished connections and influence. His older brother was Sir William Whitmore, Member of Parliament and Master of the Haberdashers and the Merchant Adventurers; his sister Elizabeth married Sir William Craven, Lord Mayor of London, and at her death in 1624 was thought to be the richest woman in England; and his nephew was Humphrey Weld the property developer. Furthermore, Whitmore's first cousin was Sir William Bond, the business associate of Anthony Smith, Henry's cousin – which connection may have drawn him into the Silver Street circle.

Though Whitmore's father had an estate in Shropshire, he was a Londoner and was apprenticed to a Haberdasher, later serving two terms as master of the Haberdashers during the 1620s. Like his fellow trustee George Lowe, he owned substantial stock in the East India Company and was a member of the Virginia Company. He became a very wealthy man, in 1631 rebuilding in the Italian style his residence near London at Balmes House, Hoxton, in the parish of Shoreditch.

On Charles I's return from Scotland in November 1641, Whitmore welcomed the king to Balmes with an elaborate display of festivities as the royal entourage processed towards the City, even having a road cut directly through his estate to smooth their journey. In 1641, he was among the aldermen who presented a petition to the king, urging him to remain near the capital.

With the outbreak of the Civil War, Whitmore's refusal to contribute to loans requested by Parliament or to pay an assessment of £1,500 set by the committee for the advance of money, led to his arrest and imprisonment in Crosby Place, Bishopsgate, place of incarceration for impenitent Royalists. His assets were seized, including rents from his properties in Essex and his East India Company stock. Whitmore died at Balmes on 12 December 1654 and was buried at St Mary Magdalen, Milk Street, London, on 6 January 1655. His will, like those of William Rolfe and Thomas Jackson, had a religious preamble, asking to receive a burial 'without pomp'. In it, he left £5 each to friends and kin, including his cousin Sir William Bond – and £10 each to four London prisons: Ludgate, Newgate, Wood Street Compter and Poultry Compter, 'for releasement of poor prisoners in them for Debt only'. He also left £20 for the maintenance of poor children in Christ's

Sir George Whitmore, painted as Master of the Haberdashers by Daniel Mytens (*c.*1590–1647). Whitmore was a very wealthy man and a prominent Royalist. At the outbreak of the Civil War his assets were seized and he was incarcerated in Crosby Place, Bishopsgate.

Hospital, £20 'to the Hospital of Bridewell and Bedlam for curing poor lunatic People and Setting loose and idle People to work' and £10 each to St Bartholomew's and St Thomas's hospitals for the curing of the sick.[23]

WILLIAM WINGFIELD
(trustee from 1619)

The third son of a prosperous sheep farmer in Lincolnshire, Wingfield was born between about 1555 and 1560, matriculating from Trinity College, Cambridge, in 1577. He first entered the household of the Devereux family as a servant of the second Earl of Essex, who was beheaded in 1601 – and by 1614 he was estate steward to the third earl. He was certainly much trusted by Essex, who, when he went abroad to fight with Protestant forces to defend the Palatinate, appointed Wingfield his deputy and principal trustee of his estates. Between 1614 and 1626, Wingfield was returned as MP for Lichfield (where Essex held the manor) on five consecutive occasions. He then went with the earl to the Essexes' estates at Chartley in Staffordshire and continued there as steward. Wingfield seems to have been a sound choice as a trustee of Smith's Charity. He was described in 1614 as 'a grave man, of much integrity and honesty' – and unlike most of the other trustees, he does not appear to have been in debt. In fact, at his death in 1639, still in the service of Essex, he left a very modest estate and in his will, after exhorting the Holy Spirit to help him achieve 'a godly, sober and righteous life', there are only two small bequests: £10 to the earl to buy a watch or ring in his memory, and £10 to the earl's housekeeper. Wingfield never married and was buried in St Clement Danes, London, in 1639.

GEORGE LOWE
(trustee from 1624 and executor of the will)

Born about 1569, in Shrewsbury, where his father was a draper, George Lowe is listed by 1609 as resident in London. As a young man he was apprenticed to John Quarles, a rich draper, and during the early 1590s worked as Quarles' factor in Stade, in Saxony.

By 1606 Lowe was back in England and running a successful cloth export business. He was engaged in a wide range of other business activities too and was involved in moneylending on a large scale. However, Lowe's decision in 1616 to pour money into a Yorkshire alum manufactory ruined him financially. Alum, a mineral dye fixative, was one of the most profitable commodities in Europe but this scheme, which attempted to extract alum from kelp, proved disastrous: not only did the experiment fail, Lowe losing thousands of pounds, but he fell foul of his associates. He was forced to call in many of his debts and to sell £2,000 worth of East India Company shares. On his return to London, he had to take up lodgings with his old friend John Kendrick, a fabulously wealthy textile merchant.

Lowe was clearly a figure of huge commercial vitality but rough around the edges, a bruiser. The court case that ensued over the alum works gives us a telling vignette of him, in which his style and behaviour is cited as a cause of conflict and that by a 'blast of his big foul mouth' and 'big roaring words' he had stirred up trouble in the workforce. Some years later, the uncle of his second wife was so appalled by the prospect of their marriage that in 1625 he tried to get an injunction to make his niece a ward of court, accusing Lowe of being 'a man much inferior to herself in quality, condition and fortune'. The marriage went ahead, however, and proved a turning point in the restoration of Lowe's fortunes. Between 1632 and 1633 he was master of the Drapers' Company and shortly after that, deputy governor of the Merchant Adventurers. In 1625, he was elected as Member of Parliament for Calne, in Wiltshire.

We do not know how Lowe encountered Henry Smith. Their paths might have crossed at various junctures: a Henry Smith is named as trading cloth with Stade in 1602. If it is our Henry then his association with George Lowe is one of the most longstanding among the trustees (and we can also add cloth trading to what we already know of his commercial enterprises). Lowe had family connections with the Wealden iron industry: his second wife, Katherine, was the widow of Sir Henry Baker of Sissinghurst Castle, a prominent figure in the industry. Other Bakers, living at Mayfield, owned the Warbleton Priory furnace. It was through this fortuitous marriage that Lowe was drawn into the orbit of the Sackvilles, kinsmen of the Bakers.

George Lowe's energy remained undimmed into old age and in 1635 (at the age of 67), he was convicted of adultery with a Mrs Smyth and fined £10. He died in 1639, a wealthy man again, leaving nearly £10,000. He was buried in the vault that he paid for in his parish church in London, St Christopher le Stocks, near Threadneedle Street, where he had been churchwarden for nearly thirty years.

SIR RICHARD GURNEY
(trustee from 1624 and executor of the will)

Sir Richard Gurney was Lowe's intimate associate: in his will, Lowe described him as 'his ancient and dear loving friend'. He was a Surrey man, born and

'Gratious Soueraigne.' A woodcut showing Sir Richard Gurney (on the left), then Lord Mayor, riding out with Sir George Whitmore to meet Charles I on the king's return to London in 1641.

baptised in the market town of Croydon on 7 April 1577, the second son of Bryan Gurney. He was apprenticed to a Clothworker, made free in 1604 and appointed a liveryman in 1611; he became master of the Clothworkers in 1633.

Some lucky breaks helped Gurney's rapid rise to wealth. In 1611, he inherited the house and business of his former master, John Colby, a silk mercer, which was said at the time to be worth £6,000; then he married Elizabeth, daughter of the wealthy Henry Sandford of Birchington, Kent. Gurney was able therefore to spend considerable time travelling, developing important future trading contacts on the Continent. He lived in great opulence, with two mansions: one in Old Jewry in the City and the other, Pointer's Grove, in Totteridge, Hertfordshire. Along the way, he acquired properties and land in London, Middlesex, Wiltshire, Sussex, and Somerset. He was elected Lord Mayor of London in 1641.

Gurney's election as Lord Mayor was rowdily contested and his Royalist sympathies set him at odds with the increasingly radical politics of the City. Gurney contributed lavishly towards the entertainment that greeted Charles as he entered London in 1641. Riding out to greet the king, he wore a robe of the 'most sumptuous crimson velvet' and was followed by 500 representatives of the Companies dressed in velvet, each attended by a footman clad in the company colours. A Royalist observer described the crowd: 'the bankes, hedges, highways, streets, stalls and windows were all embroidered with millions of people, of all sorts and fashions' that lined the royal route. There was a feast at Guildhall ('no cost was spared') and then the royal entourage made its way to Whitehall to the accompanying music of trumpets, sackbuts, cornets and the bells ringing from 121 London churches.[24]

Gurney was not a wholly uncritical supporter of the Crown, however, especially as he sought to strike a balance between loyalty to his King and the maintenance of order in the City. Nonetheless, he was ousted in the coup that secured London for Parliament in July 1642 and impeached that month for 'executing the Commission of Array against Parliament, also for framing two false and scandalous petitions to set division between King and Parliament and Parliament and the City'. He spent the rest of his life (fifteen years) in solitary confinement in the Tower. In 1646, there were reports in court that he still obstinately refused to pay his £5,000 fine.

Richard Gurney was another close associate of the Sackvilles. During his time in the Tower, the management of his own financial affairs became ever more entangled with the legacy of the third Earl of Dorset and his creditors piled in. When he made his will in 1647 he expounded in it at length on his work as a trustee for Henry Smith, pointing out that the management of his own financial affairs would have been more efficient had he not given so much of his time to the charity:

> For the better performance of the charitable uses by him intended and appointed to be performed whereupon I have intermeddled as feoffee [trustee] and Executor amongst many others and have taken much care and pains for the performance of the said trust and confidence for twenty years together more last past or thereabouts to my extreme trouble and damage diverting me from the necessary care and managing of my own Estate.

After his death in 1657 Gurney's estate paid a high price for his Royalist sympathies and losses were recorded that may have been as high as £40,000. David Lloyd, a later Royalist hagiographer, described in glowing terms Gurney's 'faithful discharge' of his trusteeship of Smith's Charity. His work in the 'buying of Impropriations, to be Legally and bona fide, laid to the Church' was presented as proof of his good character: Lloyd, a committed Anglican, was keen to distance Smith's Charity from any taint of puritanism, stressing further that Gurney was buried in St Lawrence Old Jewry in London, with three 'Orthodox' priests in attendance and with the 'Liturgy' (that is, the Anglican Rite according to the Book of Common Prayer, which had been proscribed by Parliament).[25]

SIR WILLIAM BLAKE
(trustee from 1624 and executor of the will)

Blake was born about 1582 in Andover, Hampshire, the son of John and Margaret Blake. He was apprenticed to the Vintners and became a freeman in 1603. By 1616, however, he was a scrivener with a shop in Fleet Street. Shortly afterwards he married Mary, the daughter of Henry Beverley of London.

Blake became a commissioner for the sale of crown lands between 1604 and 1608, and a member of a syndicate (with Peter Vanlore and Lawrence Baskerville) to contract for the sale of crown rectories and tithes. On the death of his father in 1606, he inherited the family's Hampshire property and six years later was able to purchase Hale House and its thirty acres in Brompton, in the parish of Kensington; he had been renting the house since 1605.

In 1616, Blake bought the ferry between Chelsea and Battersea but the business failed. The marriage of his son in 1624 to the daughter of Thomas Hawker of Heytesbury may have been an attempt to bail himself out of his financial difficulties. He bought Heytesbury Manor from Hawker for £11,500, a price partially offset by the £3,000 that was Miss Hawker's dowry.[26] Blake became Member of Parliament for Heytesbury in 1626 and was knighted the following year. From then on, his business fortunes were tied closely to his nephew and apprentice, William Rolfe – whose activities were in turn tied closely to the fortunes of Henry Smith and his charitable foundation.

In 1626, Blake bought an office in the Court of Common Pleas that yielded him £700 per annum. But to raise the £10,000 purchase price he sold two manors to Rolfe, including Heytesbury, and mortgaged most of the rest of his property. Rolfe then defaulted on his payments, and though Blake accepted promissory notes, this was a bad mistake: late Chancery suits were to estimate Rolfe's debts as £30,000 and after Blake's death, there were years of litigation (lasting until 1660), in which his widow petitioned Rolfe for restitution of her jointure lands and other estates.[27]

Blake died intestate at Hale House on 30 October 1630 and was buried in St Mary Abbots, Kensington, on 2 November. An entry in the parish register records that he was 'a religious, charitable, good friend to this Church and Parish'. A memorial tablet (no longer there) to Blake in the church exhorted the visitor to pause and reflect on his virtues: 'Stay, Reader, gaze, admire and pass not slightly o'er.' Blake had also been a close associate of Baptist Hicks, Viscount Campden, who had in 1608 purchased the manor at Chipping Campden from Antony Smith, and he was a trustee of the small charity that Hicks founded for the 'good and benefit' of the poor in Kensington. Blake also paid for the iron frame which held the hour-glass on the pulpit in the church. Soon after his death, the trustees of Smith's Charity, at the urging of William Rolfe, purchased several parcels of Blake's diminished Brompton estate. It was to become the charity's best-known and most lucrative asset.

WILLIAM ROLFE
(trustee from 1626 and executor of the will)

William Rolfe is one of the more intriguing of the Smith's trustees and the one of whom we have the clearest evidence of his closeness to Henry Smith. Rolfe's money-making activities, many of them if not illegal certainly risky, shed light on the labyrinthine business dealings that underpinned the wealth of Henry Smith and the men who owed him money. He was born about 1594 and yet he seems to have become at a very young age the old man's most trusted associate.

While still a young man, Rolfe acquired a considerable property portfolio, sailing close to the wind on several transactions. He came from a yeoman family of 'mean estate' in Hampshire. But after his fortunes were boosted by an advantageous marriage in 1619 to Sarah Deane, a Kent heiress, he began speculating in property, snapping up pockets of land all over the country. These included, for £600, a manor in Wales from his sister-in-law, three Wiltshire manors, large properties in Hampshire and the leases of two coalmines in Yorkshire and Warwickshire. In 1619, for £850, he acquired the 'parcel of land called the Broad' in Hellingly, Oxfordshire – purchased from the third Earl of Dorset and his kinsman Edward Sackville.[28] In 1624, Rolfe is listed as living in the Inner Temple and is there recorded as 'citizen and Vintner'.[29]

He worked closely with his uncle Sir William Blake, a Vintner, and was bound apprentice to him, becoming in 1614 a freeman of the Vintners. In 1610, aged 16, Rolfe was described on a bond as 'servant' to Blake in his scrivener's shop in Fleet Street (in this case the definition of servant being closer to apprentice). In 1619, Blake and Rolfe were involved in a dispute over the recovery of land in Norfolk that was owing to them.[30] In 1626, Rolfe purchased from his uncle the manor of Heytesbury in Wiltshire and in 1628 was returned there as Member of Parliament, as Blake had been before him.

Evidence of Rolfe's business dealings – property transactions, moneylending and litigation – is legion. The surviving documentation shows him associated through business with a wide range of Henry Smith's circle, including the Throckmortons, the Sackvilles (particularly Edward Lindsey, an executor of the third earl's estate) and his brother-in-law (and creditor) John Goodwin, who later leased the Warbleton estate from the Smith's trustees. In 1635, he sold the manor of Stoughton in Leicestershire to the charity – which brought in revenues of £220 per annum.

Rolfe's intimacy with Henry Smith may have been distrusted by his fellow trustees. In 1638, in the early years of the charity, Richard Gurney and George Lowe sued Rolfe, claiming that he had been detaining sums from Henry's personal estate for his own uses, although we only have their side of the story.

Yet it was Rolfe who can be held at least partly responsible for the charity's religious benefactions. Like his fellow Puritan Henry Jackson, Rolfe's presence in the last years of Henry's life influenced the charity's bequests to the poor clergy, the interest in the model town of Dorchester and the donation to the Feoffees of Impropriations. William Rolfe died in 1646, leaving his executors to settle his debts by the sale of numerous of his landholdings all over the country.

SIR CHRISTOPHER NEVILL
(trustee from 1624 and executor of the will)

Like Richard Amherst, Sir Christopher Nevill came from Lewes in Sussex and is another Sackville connection profiting from the extravagances of the third Earl of Dorset: in 1623, he purchased from him Sheffield Park in Sussex for £3,000. His elder brother Henry married the daughter of the first earl.

Nevill was born about 1578, the second surviving son of Lord Bergavenny, whose family were prominent figures during the reigns of Henry VIII and his heirs; his great-grandfather was the Duke of Buckingham who was executed for treason in 1521. By 1608, Nevill had married Mary Darcy, one of the five daughters and co-heirs of Thomas Darcy of Tolleshunt D'Arcy in Essex. This was the 290-acre Essex estate that Nevill acquired on the death of his father-in-law and which in 1636 he was to dispose of to the Smith's Charity in settlement of his debts to Henry Smith; it was listed as bringing in revenues of £140 per annum.

Nevill was returned as Member of Parliament for Lewes in 1614 and on 3 June of that year made an impassioned speech against James I's increasing demands for money: 'O tempora! O mores! O miserable times, when we see the Commonwealth to groan under more grievous taxations than ever were, contrary to all old and modern examples.' When later he blamed the king for the dissolution of Parliament, he was consigned to the Tower for five days.

Nevill's Sackville connections proved useful – to both parties. While in Parliament, he was appointed to consider the bill to endow Sackville College, the almshouses in East Grinstead, in accordance with the will of the second Earl of Dorset; in 1616, the third earl and his brother Sir Edward Sackville gave evidence in the Star Chamber on behalf of Nevill when he was beaten up in Lincoln's Inn Fields by men employed by the jealous husband of Nevill's mistress – and he was awarded £500 damages. In 1621, Nevill spoke up for a bill to sever the entail on the estate of Sir Richard Lumley, another Smith's Charity trustee.

When his father died in 1622, Nevill inherited the manor of Newton St Loe in Somerset and lived there for most of the rest of his life. His material fortunes dwindled and by the time of his death in February 1649, he was living in cramped lodgings in Covent Garden, London. He left only a verbal will and on his deathbed it was reported that he sent for his grandchild Mary Nevill and taking her by the hand said: 'This is my dear grandchild and whom I intended a good portion. It being all my worldly business to make her a fortune but these times have much hindered me in what I intended, but I freely and absolutely give her all that I have both plate, money and goods and whatsoever is mine that I have power to give.'

RICHARD LUMLEY
(trustee from 1619)

Richard Lumley, later first Viscount Lumley, appears to have been close to Henry at the time of his death – and furthermore indebted to him to the tune of £1,000. It was his kinsman, Lord Lumley, who sold the Gloucestershire estate at Longney to Henry Smith in 1591. Like William Rolfe, Lumley was nearly forty years Henry's junior.

Richard Lumley was baptised at Chester-le-Street, Co. Durham, on 7 April 1589, the son of Roger Lumley. However, he owed his later position to his kinsman John Lumley, third Baron Lumley, who passed over his closest heirs in favour of Richard, who thus inherited mines at Lumley and Chester-le-Street, the manor of Hartlepool in Co. Durham, and, in Sussex, an estate at Stansted, near Chichester.

It made him a rich man: at the time of his death the Durham coal mines alone brought in revenues of £1,040 per annum.[31] It is less clear whether he also inherited John's Catholicism. John had been concerned that Richard should be educated as a true Catholic, and Richard's grandson was also raised a Catholic in his lifetime. But Richard's own religion remains mysterious, and it is most likely that he conformed, perhaps nominally, to the Church of England.

Richard Lumley's first marriage, to Frances, widow of William Holland of Chichester and daughter of Henry Shelley of Warminghurst, further entrenched him in Sussex society. In 1616 he was knighted, and on 12 July 1628 created Viscount Lumley of Waterford. He evidently much preferred living in the south. In January 1638, as war approached between Charles I and his Scottish subjects, Lumley was ordered to leave his Sussex estates and return to Lumley Castle. At the time of his will, he regarded Stansted as his main seat.

In the 1620s, Lumley owed Henry Smith £1,000. In 1639 he was at odds with another leading figure in Sussex, John Ashburnham, over a lease and mortgage, in a business that left the latter fuming over the 'unworthy delays of Lord Lumley, a person of so much craft and so little honesty'. Moreover, his second marriage in 1630, to Elizabeth, daughter of Sir William Cornwallis of Brome, Suffolk, and widow of Sir William Sandys of Mottisfont, Hampshire, involved him in settling the debts that she owed to the Earl of Danby. Yet by March 1640 relations with his wife had fallen apart, and he was complaining to the king he was afraid that, 'differences since growing between him and his wife, just satisfaction [in the Danby business] is denied him'.

During the Civil War Lumley garrisoned Lumley Castle for the king. He later claimed that though he had left Stansted in January 1644 to join the king, he had never taken up arms against Parliament. Nevertheless, in late summer 1645 he was president of Rupert's council of war just before the prince surrendered Bristol. Lumley came to terms with the new regimes. His composition fine was in time reduced to £1,925 15s. At the Restoration he put his name to a declaration by moderate Royalists not to take revenge on their old enemies.

Lumley was the second-longest surviving of all Henry's trustees. He died between 13 April 1661 (when he made his will) and 12 March 1663 (when it was proved). At the time of his will he was leasing from the Smith trustees the manor of Longstock Harrington, in Hampshire, which he had in fact sold to them. He is buried in the vault of Cheam parish church. Lumley was succeeded by his grandson, Richard, later the first Earl of Scarbrough – in 1688, he was one of the seven who wrote to William III inviting him to come to England.

SIR GEORGE CROKE
(trustee from 1624 and executor of the will)

George Croke, born in 1560, was the third son of Sir John Croke of Chilton, Buckinghamshire. In 1575, he was admitted to the Inner Temple and in 1584 called to the Bar. With the profits from a lucrative legal practice, he purchased estates in Buckinghamshire and Oxfordshire and in 1610 married Mary, the daughter of Sir Thomas Bennet, a Lord Mayor. The marriage 'fell out unexpected to his friends that conceived a purpose in him never to have married'; his wife was 20 years of agc and Croke was described as 'an ancient bachelor' of 50. For all this (and perhaps because of it) he had a reputation as a 'worthie' figure, praised by his contemporaries for his wisdom, probity and civic virtue.

He was made a serjeant-at-law in 1623 (he had earlier refused the position rather than pay the king for the office) and in 1625 was appointed a Justice in the Court of Common Pleas, transferring to the King's Bench three years later, by which time he was in his sixties. In his twelve years of service there, he was regarded as a man of both principle and integrity. He was one of the few judges critical of the king's un-parliamentary financial measures, especially ship money, giving only qualified approval when Charles sought the judges' ruling on his right to demand financial aid from his subjects in time of danger. Although he had to yield to majority opinion, he staunchly held that the exacting of ship money contravened the statute and common law of England, by which a man had a freedom and property in his goods and estate that could be taken from him only with his personal consent, or by his consent as expressed in Parliament. At the trial of the politician John Hampden, who had refused to pay ship money (one of the sparks of revolution), Croke vigorously spoke out in his defence and was one of only two judges who ruled against its lawfulness. According to Thomas Fuller's *Worthies of England*, a common saying at the time was that 'The King has ship money by hook but not by Croke.'

George Croke lived to a great age, dying in 1642 in his eighties. He was suffering from painful gout but was still a figure of substantial political reputation. He was described by a contemporary as 'of puritan persuasion and party' and in his will, he stressed that his funeral should have no 'heraldry', 'hearse' nor 'unnecessary ceremonies'. He is buried in Waterstock, in Oxfordshire, where there is a monument in the parish church that lauds his modest demeanour, his goodness to the poor and his sound religious principles. The almshouses that he bequeathed to the nearby village of Horton-cum-Studley are still there today.

SIR HENRY HENN (OR HENE)
(appointed trustee in the will to replace Edward Francis)

In his will, Henry Smith made a passing reference to 'Henry Henn, gent, sometimes my servant' – which probably means that Henn was Henry's former apprentice. Henn is one of the trustees introduced on the 1626 deed and seems to have been intimately connected with Henry.

There is no record of his birth but Henry (or 'Harry') Henn was described as aged 88 in the Berkshire Visitations of 1665 – which would put the date at some time in 1576 or 1577. He was the second son of William and Anne Henn of Dorking, Surrey. According to the certificate accompanying his Grant of Arms in 1642, there were Henns originally from Wales who 'were gentlemen of good note and of Coat Armour from whom it may probably be supposed the said Sir Henry Henn alias Hene to be descended'.[32] At some point, Henn married Dorothy Stapleford of Hertfordshire. This may not have been his first marriage or it may have been an unusually late one: at any rate, his eldest son was born in 1632 when Henn was nearly 60 years old.

Henn (who displayed a talent for political survival) enjoyed a number of Crown appointments and privileges. He established himself near Windsor and was drawn to the Court, and as early as 1608, aged about 30, Henn was awarded the profits of fines on Catholic recusants in Staffordshire. By 1630, he had been appointed a Serjeant (officer in charge) of the Carriages in the royal household. In 1628, he was Bailiff Itinerant in Chester and in 1639, he and his brother Hugh were given the keepership of the Queen's garden at Greenwich – which came with a fee of four pence a day for sixty years. In 1642, he became a baronet.

Henn acquired crown property at Winkfield, Berkshire, the manor of Folly John (or Foliejohn), 'with the woods and deer on the payment of £3,400 and reservation of a yearly rent of £10 to the Crown'.[33] In 1643, he was assessed for tax in two residences: Folly John and a house in the parish of St Martin-in-the-Fields, London.

Although his fortunes prospered under the Crown, Henry Henn seems to have navigated the choppy waters of the English Civil War with some skill. Unlike his brother Hugh, who not only attended Charles at Oxford in 1644 but was taken prisoner at the Battle of Naseby and then went on to forfeit much of his property, Henn retained a careful neutrality, which was rewarded in 1651 by his appointment as High Sheriff of Berkshire.

From 1610 onwards, there are records of a large number of property transactions in which Henn had an involvement: in that year he was named in a complicated deal over the Pulteney estate in Westminster, in what is now modern Piccadilly. In 1654, in the first years of the Commonwealth, he petitioned to buy the gardens at Greenwich.

Henn was the longest-lived of all the first Smith's Charity trustees, outliving the others by many years, a remarkable survivor. He died at some point between

The monument to Sir George Croke in the church at Waterstock, Oxfordshire. Croke is shown in his judge's robes and his brave stand against Ship Money is described in the panel below the figure.

15 February 1666 (when he made his will) and 1 May 1668 (when it was proved). At the Restoration in 1660, Charles II appointed him to his old office of Serjeant of the Carriages, a move resented by the other incumbent of the role, Allen Lockhart, who stressed his own Royalist credentials, pointing out that he had attended King Charles I at Oxford when Henn had declined to. He complained that Henn's 'great age renders him incapable of service' and hoped that the King might see fit to pension him off.[34]

HENRY JACKSON
(nephew, trustee from 1626 and an overseer of the will)

Henry Jackson, younger son of Joan Jackson, is the Jackson who has the most bearing on the legacy of his uncle, Henry Smith. He was a member of the Grocers' Company.

There are strong indications that the Jackson family, like William Rolfe, had Puritan leanings.

A PURITAN FAMILY.

We do not know Henry Smith's precise religious affiliations, but there is evidence that he had some sympathy with Puritanism. Certainly the Jackson family, the children of his sister, Joan, had many links to prominent Puritans.

Henry Jackson in 1650, the year of his death, left a will to which he had given a strikingly Puritan preamble and in which he asked 'to be made a partaker of the Kingdom of Heaven with the Elect in Christ'.

Henry Jackson clearly had his poor kindred in mind in his own will: he left £25 a year for twelve years 'to be bestowed by my wife and daughter according to their discretions upon the poor, needy members of Christ of my kindred or others that shall be prisoners or any other poverty, distress or want'.[35] He also specifically bequeathed to his son-in-law William Spurstowe, his daughter Sarah's husband, a copy of Foxe's *Book of Martyrs*, that definitive work of Protestant martyrology.

> Item I give and bequeath to my loving son in law doctor William Spurstowe either my Book of Martyrs and my great faire bible with the large margin or else in case he shall like better of it six of my best books in my study to be of his own election. Item I entreat and desire my Executrix to bestow Parte of my household goods when she gives over housekeeping unto and amongst my kindred according as she shall think most fitting and I will and desire my executrix to be ready to give account when she shall be called thereunto of all monies by me received and paid in relation to the state of my deceased Uncle Henry Smith disposed to charitable uses.*

The presence of Dr Spurstowe among the younger Jacksons' connections throws an interesting sidelight on the tumultuous sectarian politics of the Civil War, commonwealth and restoration eras. Spurstowe was the rector of Hackney, to the east of London, where he built six almshouses; he was a prominent Presbyterian and one of the best-known Protestant preachers of the day, the author of scores of published polemics, sermons and devotional works.

GEORGE DUNCOMB
(an overseer of the will)

The Duncombs were an established Surrey family with close associations with the Wealden iron industry. The first wife of Smith's trustee George Lowe

* Henry had himself been bequeathed the very same copy of Foxe's *Book of Martyrs* by his nephew and namesake, who died in 1647.

The memorial to George Duncomb in the old parish church in Albury, where the Duncombs owned the estate. (The faint figure on the wall depicts St Christopher.)

was the widow of William Duncomb, George's brother, so this association may have provided George Duncomb's link to Henry Smith. He was born about 1564, the son of Roger Duncomb, in Shalford, Surrey, and later was called to the bar, found himself influential connections at Court and seems to have acquired a large fortune in landholdings using his training in law and conveyancing.

At the time of his death he owned properties in Merrow, Shalford, Tanley and Albury, all in Surrey, retaining as his main seat the manor of Albury Weston, which he had purchased in 1610. He had also owned the manor of Poyle, near Guildford, sold to Henry Smith in 1603. Rents from the manor of Poyle were allocated to Guildford by Henry's gift. Duncomb acted as steward at Bramley Court from 1617 until his death.

In 1604 he bought the manor of Burningfold, with its ironworks, for £886, only to find that John Middleton claimed a right to the estate – so Duncomb sold his rights to Middleton and two others four years later. He died in 1646 and he and his wife, Judith (of another large Surrey dynasty, the Carrills of Wonersh, who were prominent Royalists), are buried in Albury church.[36]

SIR ROBERT PARKHURST
(an overseer of the will)

Robert Parkhurst, who was born in 1569, came from another Surrey yeoman family. The Parkhursts had strong links with Guildford: Robert's father Henry was a mercer there and his uncle Thomas was several times the town's mayor. He married Eleanor Babington, who came from Chorley in Surrey.

Parkhurst was a member of the Clothworker's Company. He had a successful career as a cloth merchant and served in several of the City's great offices: as Sheriff of London (1624–5), as Alderman (Portsoken Ward 1624–34, and then Bread Street Ward until his death) and as Lord Mayor (1634–5). He lived in Cheapside, London, and in the country, in Surrey, having in 1628 acquired substantial estates in Pyrford. That year, his links with Henry Smith may have been cemented when Robert Parkhurst the younger married Elizabeth, the daughter of Sir Robert Baker of Sissinghurst, the stepson of George Lowe.

With Parkhurst's death on 19 October 1636, his will drew the net of connections to the Smith trustees tighter. Parkhurst's brother-in-law, overseer

An eighteenth-century depiction of Spurstowe's Almshouses, Hackney. William Spurstowe, a well-known Puritan preacher, was married to Henry's great-niece Sarah Jackson and was also related to Sir Robert Parkhurst, the overseer of Henry's will. He was the rector of Hackney and his almshouses stand (in a modern form) to this day.

The tomb of Sir Robert Parkhurst in Holy Trinity Church, Guildford, shows him wearing the chain of his office as the town's mayor.

of his will, was the London merchant William Spurstowe, husband of his sister Damaris and father of the preacher who would marry Henry's great-niece Sarah Jackson. In its preamble, Parkhurst's will displays a strong Puritanism, an assurance that he was among the elect:

> I commend my Soul into the hands of Almighty God trusting and assuredly believing that only by the merits of the precious death and passion of my Lord and Saviour Jesus Christ, I shall obtain full and free pardon, remission and forgiveness of all my sins and shall enjoy everlasting life in the Kingdom of Heaven among the elect children of God.

Parkhurst also left £5 apiece for ten 'godly and conformable preachers' to be selected by his executors; and another £5 each for the care of ten preachers' widows who are left poor and distressed being godly, as well as £100 for the relief of 'the poor children harboured in Christ's Hospital in London' adding that 'and my will and mind is that a convenient number of the said children shall accompany my body to my burial'. He also left £40 to pay for a dinner 'for the governors of Christ's and of the other hospitals, who shall accompany my body to my burial'; £100 went towards the maintenance of the poor in Bridewell; there was also money for and towards releasing poor prisoners for small debts and £20 each for the relief of the inmates of several London prisons.

The people of Surrey were taken care of too: Parkhurst gave various small benefactions to villages in the region of his estates at Pyrford and Ripley. Mr Bray, the curate at Pyrford, received £5 and for the Pyrford parish poor, the sum of three pound six shillings and eight pence 'to be distributed amongst them' and another £6 6s 4d 'to be kept in Stock to Maintain the poor to work that there be no beggar in Pyrford'. Further sums were to be distributed to the poor of Ripley who were deemed 'honest and impotent'.[38]

5

The Early Years

The trustees' first action, following Henry's death, was to establish his public credentials as a leading philanthropist by commissioning a handsome wall monument in stone to commemorate him in Wandsworth church. Set against the chancel wall to the north of the altar, it is framed by ionic columns supporting an architrave. Above it two cherubs flank a cartouche in which Henry's coat of arms displays the fess between two saltires that can also be seen in the arms of his kinsman Sir Thomas Smith. The (rather youthful looking) bearded figure portrayed on the monument is the only known likeness of Henry – if likeness it is, for, like Henry's will, it sticks to conventions. In his ruff and alderman's robes, he is depicted holding a memento mori in the shape of a skull and kneeling at a prayer desk. Below the monument is a panel that praises its subject's philanthropic benefactions (the date used for his death being taken from the old Julian calendar and therefore given as 1627).

Shortly after Henry's death, Henry Jackson moved into his uncle's Silver Street house and the trustees began the process of creating Smith's Charity – as Henry had planned it. The first task was to add to its landholdings by purchasing the rectory at Alfriston and part of the tithes of Mayfield, both in Sussex, in 1629. The rents from these estates were to go to fulfil the bequest to the poor clergy.

The establishment of a viable charitable enterprise was not plain sailing, however. Eleven months after Henry died, Richard Amherst filed a Complaint, in which he claimed that he should not be required to repay his £1,000 debt as he considered it fully redeemed by the tireless work he had put in over the years for the benefit of both Henry and his charity – and for which he had never received a penny in recompense. Amherst even stipulated in his will in 1630 that his executors were not to repay the loan. 'I will and devise that if I happen to die before all the money which I owe upon bonds or other specialties be paid within the sum of two hundred pounds except my debt to Mr Henry Smith deceased which debt I have painfully deserved at his hands and much more and therefore I take no care in conscience that the said debt should be paid.'[38]

For forty years, Amherst wrote in his Complaint, he was the 'familiar acquaintance' to whom Henry entrusted most of the legal operations of his business affairs including, among countless transactions and lawsuits, a 'long and tedious suit' with the tenants of Longney, several suits related to the estate of the third Earl of Dorset and an ongoing battle of suits and counter-suits with the Stollion family, from whom Henry had received Iwood Place at Warbleton and the Rushlake Furnace in payment for a £10,000 mortgage unpaid by Sir Thomas Stollion; he had also been entrusted with the running of the Sussex estates – the labour of which had, he claimed, been to the detriment of his own business. In addition to all this, Amherst reminded the trustees that he had attended Henry constantly at Silver Street in his last years; he had been at the old man's beck and call 'by day and night, being sent for not only in vacation time, or two or three days a week in term time and

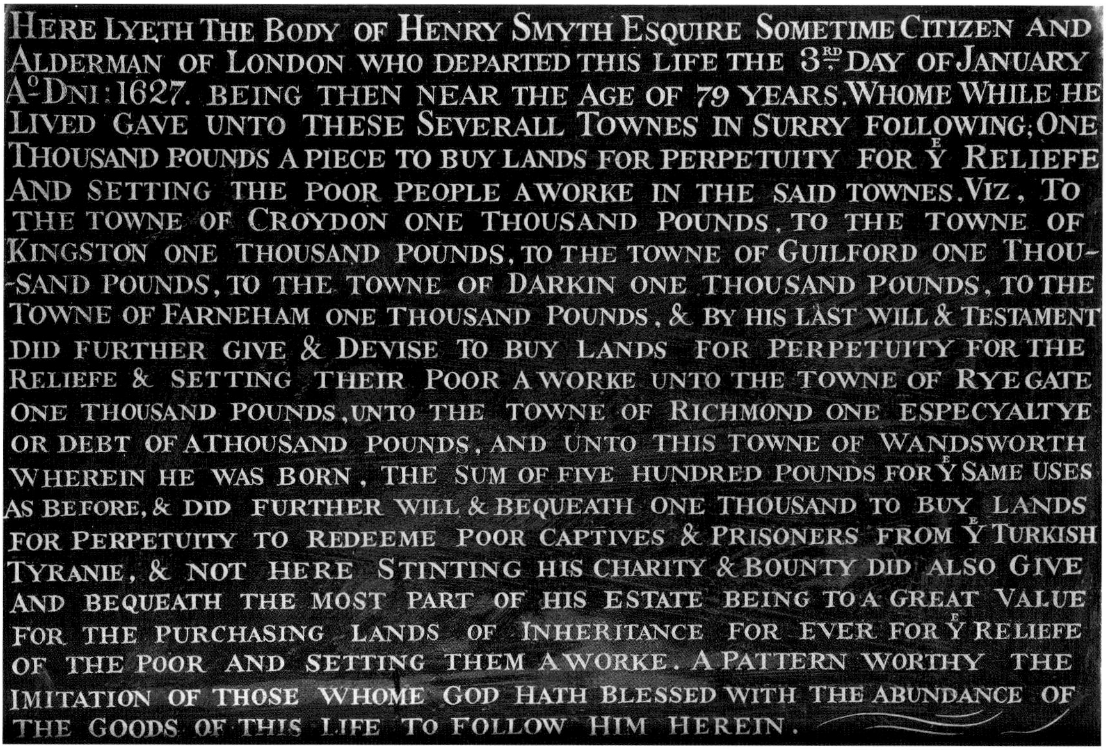

HERE LYETH THE BODY OF HENRY SMYTH ESQUIRE SOMETIME CITIZEN AND
ALDERMAN OF LONDON WHO DEPARTED THIS LIFE THE 3RD DAY OF JANUARY
Aº DNI: 1627. BEING THEN NEAR THE AGE OF 79 YEARS. WHOME WHILE HE
LIVED GAVE UNTO THESE SEVERALL TOWNES IN SURRY FOLLOWING; ONE
THOUSAND POUNDS A PIECE TO BUY LANDS FOR PERPETUITY FOR YE RELIEFE
AND SETTING THE POOR PEOPLE AWORKE IN THE SAID TOWNES. VIZ, TO
THE TOWNE OF CROYDON ONE THOUSAND POUNDS, TO THE TOWNE OF
KINGSTON ONE THOUSAND POUNDS, TO THE TOWNE OF GUILFORD ONE THOU-
-SAND POUNDS, TO THE TOWNE OF DARKIN ONE THOUSAND POUNDS, TO THE
TOWNE OF FARNEHAM ONE THOUSAND POUNDS, & BY HIS LAST WILL & TESTAMENT
DID FURTHER GIVE & DEVISE TO BUY LANDS FOR PERPETUITY FOR THE
RELIEFE & SETTING THEIR POOR A WORKE UNTO THE TOWNE OF RYEGATE
ONE THOUSAND POUNDS, UNTO THE TOWNE OF RICHMOND ONE ESPECYALTYE
OR DEBT OF A THOUSAND POUNDS, AND UNTO THIS TOWNE OF WANDSWORTH
WHEREIN HE WAS BORN, THE SUM OF FIVE HUNDRED POUNDS FOR YE SAME USES
AS BEFORE, & DID FURTHER WILL & BEQUEATH ONE THOUSAND TO BUY LANDS
FOR PERPETUITY TO REDEEME POOR CAPTIVES & PRISONERS FROM YE TURKISH
TYRANIE, & NOT HERE STINTING HIS CHARITY & BOUNTY DID ALSO GIVE
AND BEQUEATH THE MOST PART OF HIS ESTATE BEING TO A GREAT VALUE
FOR THE PURCHASING LANDS OF INHERITANCE FOR EVER FOR YE RELIEFE
OF THE POOR AND SETTING THEM AWORKE. A PATTERN WORTHY THE
IMITATION OF THOSE WHOME GOD HATH BLESSED WITH THE ABUNDANCE OF
THE GOODS OF THIS LIFE TO FOLLOW HIM HEREIN.

Below Henry Smith's monument in Wandsworth is inscribed a list of his bequests, including the £1000 apiece that he gave to the Surrey towns of Reigate, Guildford, Kingston, Dorking, Farnham and Croydon. The £500 he left to Wandsworth seems to have disappeared at some point over the following century.

sometimes more, and often to stay with him long after term time and divers times came up to London from his home forty miles away.'[39]

A glimpse of Henry's controlling flintiness in money matters is afforded by a stinging detail in Amherst's Complaint – still bitterly recollected after thirty-five years. Amherst had, he wrote, acted as broker for Henry in 1602, for the purchase of the Longney and Eastbrooke estates. In these transactions he had negotiated with another lawyer, one Mr Baber of Lincoln's Inn; Amherst had twice had to pay Baber £10 for the delivery of the requisite documents to George Whitmore on behalf of Henry – and he had never been paid back, Henry insisting that paying Baber was Amherst's mistake and the documents were Henry's by right. Henry would often go at night, wrote Amherst, to visit the Earl of Dorset (Richard, the third earl) and usually called on Amherst to accompany him. Amherst, on several occasions, had asked Henry to recompense him 'in full for his labours and expenses to which Smith would reply that he would do so . . . and that he were worse than a beast if he should not well consider of his friends for all their pains and friendship towards him'.[40]

The other trustees also squabbled among themselves. George Whitmore had resigned as executor of the will shortly after Henry's death, hardly surprising as he had had the contentious matter of Amherst's debt to deal with. In 1638, Richard Gurney and George Lowe accused William Rolfe of fraud, alleging that he was withholding money from the Smith estate and using it to feather his own nest; it was a matter that appears to have been left unresolved. When Gurney wrote his will in 1647, while incarcerated in the Tower of London, he claimed that as the only surviving executor of the will (with Henry Jackson) there were concerns that the proper purposes of the charity would be 'suppressed, neglected or misgoverned' owing to poor governance by certain trustees: he was particularly anxious that his heirs should not be laid open to 'trouble and danger' in the years to come. Warning that the charity's paperwork, its 'evidences, books and writings' should be closely scrutinised and at the earliest opportunity removed to a safe place, Gurney also recommended that Smith's Charity turn over its administration, by Act of Parliament, to Christ's Hospital, of which he had been governor, which would see to it that 'the true intention of the said Henry Smith' was honoured.

Despite the infighting, there is evidence that the charity started to distribute payments to its chosen parishes quickly after Henry's death: in Surrey, they received their grants within three or four years. The earliest evidence we have found comes from Lambeth where, on 20 November 1630, the churchwardens recorded:

> Rec [eived] . . . of one Jackson dwelling in Silver Street being one of Mr Smith deceased ['s executors] the sum of five pounds due at the feasts of St Michael last past for one half year being the one half moiety of the yearly revenue Mr Smith to the poor of Lambeth for ever to be paid at the two feasts, of St Michael [30 September] and the Annunciation of the Blessed Virgin Mary [25 March] by equal portions to be disposed to the use of the poor of Lambeth as his executors shall appoint and it is ordered by his will that this shall not be any ease or help to the parishioners of their yearly tax [i.e. the poor rate] but to be disposed of by other helps for the poor viz as placing forth poor children or the like.

The winter of 1630–1 was a hard one, as a bad harvest had sent the price of grain and bread soaring. Accordingly, seven weeks later, on 9 January, the parish vestry – with the consent of the executor, surely Henry Jackson – broke the strict terms of the Smith bequest to meet urgent local needs. To this end, the churchwardens were empowered to make cash payments to the poor where they saw most need, 'it being a dear year of corn'. A host of small payments were made between 12 January and 3 April. The first known recipients of Smith's Charity were therefore Goody Ingrom and Wells of Kennington, who received two shillings and one shilling respectively. 'Goody' implies a married woman rather than a widow, but there is no evidence of a husband present to help with the maintenance of her children. Hers is a bleak story. Between 12 January and 5 February she received in all twelve shillings at five different times: eighteen pence was for a nurse-keeper for herself, whilst there were two payments of two shillings for the weekly nursing of her child. On 11 February, six shillings and four pence was paid for the disposal of her body while the children were 'put to keep' in the families of neighbours. On 28 March, a further payment of nine shillings was made to help the Ingrom family: 'To Goody Parker for keeping Goody Ingrom's girl till it died'.

> To Goody Ingrom for a shroud xviii d.; to four men sent to bring her to Church xvid.; to the men that loaded her goods to the cart vid.; for bringing away the goods xiid.; for the women that keep the Children for meat for them iis.; which children were put to keep upon Friday the xith of February 1630, the one to Mercer, the other to Marmaduke Parker.

The payments made from Smith's £10 in the early months of 1631 were spread over a range of recipients and needs: for instance, two shillings to 'lame Zachary being sick'; one shilling to 'Jellyes wife childbed' and one shilling and sixpence to 'Old Rich for making clean the streets' are among the many recipients. On 3 April, one shilling was given to 'the poor at the church door'. Some of the needy recognised in Lambeth were more transient poor, who also stood outside the strict terms of Henry's bequest. The churchwardens gave sixpence to 'a poor man and woman with letters testimonial' (that is, they were authorised to travel collecting alms). Another sixpence went to 'a soldier directed to me

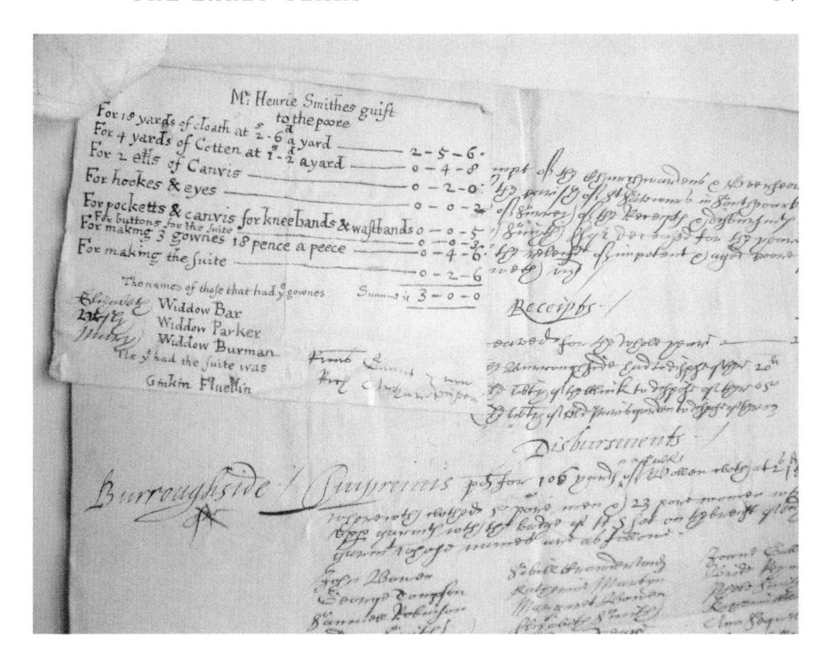
Mr Henrie Smithes guift
to the poore
For 18 yards of cloath at 2s-6d a yard ——— 2-5-6
For 4 yards of Cotten at 1s-2d ayard ——— 0-4-8
For 2 ells of Canvis ——— 0-2-0
For hookes & eyes ——— 0-0-2
For pocketts & canvis for kneebands & wastbands 0-0-5
For buttons for the suite ——— 0-0-3
For making 3 gownes 18 pence a peece ——— 0-4-6
For making the suite ——— 0-2-6
Summe is 3-0-0

The names of those that had ye gownes
Widdow Bar
Widdow Parker
Widdow Burman
He yt had the suite was
Gwkin Fluellin

Receipts

Disbursments

Boroughside

This example of Henry's gift is in the parish records of St Saviour, Southwark, and is dated 1631.

by Doctor Featley' (Daniel Featley was the rector of the parish).

Later, outside the crisis year, Lambeth used the charity money more in line with Henry's will: for providing clothes for the poor. In the nearby parish of St Thomas, Southwark, the parish commemorated the first year of Smith's gift, 1632, with a table on the wall recording the recipients, all given coats with Smith's initials on them, that were paid for by Henry Smith's £4. 'The Yearly Gift of Four Pounds, given by Master Henry Smith Esq; to this Parish of St Thomas, hath been dispended on the Poor this year past, in manner and form following. In witness thereof, we the Minister, Churchwardens, and Overseers, have subscribed our names.' Below it, we learn that five parishioners, three women and two men, ranging in age from 34 years to 95, had received garments costing an average of eighteen shillings each.

Next door to St Thomas, was the church of St Saviour, Southwark, which was given £28 a year by Smith's Charity.* It was a very big parish: the largest of its three divisions, Boroughside, contained in the 1630s nearly 1,000 households. It was the parish where the Globe Theatre was situated, but was as well known then as a parish of both poverty and industry. There were many pensioners dependent on parish relief every year, but in the hard year of 1631 the churchwardens' accounts painted an even grimmer picture: some 600 families were 'relieved at certain times when it is thought most needful'.

As in Lambeth and St Thomas, Southwark, the provision of clothing loomed large. In 1639, the Boroughside officers bought '106 yards & a half of Woollen cloth at 2s 1d the yard Wherewith clothed 5 poor men & 23 pore women with upper garments with the badge of HS set on the breast of each garment'. In a neighouring division, the Liberty of the Old Paris Garden, the officers bought '18 yards of Cloth at 2s 6d the yard wherewith made a suite for one poor man & 3 gowns for 3 poore widows with the badge of HS on the suit'. But in St Saviour, money was also spent on apprenticing poor children, such as, in 1633, 'Barbarie Lane found in Maide Lane Ditch'. In 1639, Boroughside also used Henry's money to bind out three boys as a basket maker, a

* St Saviour was later to become Southwark Cathedral.

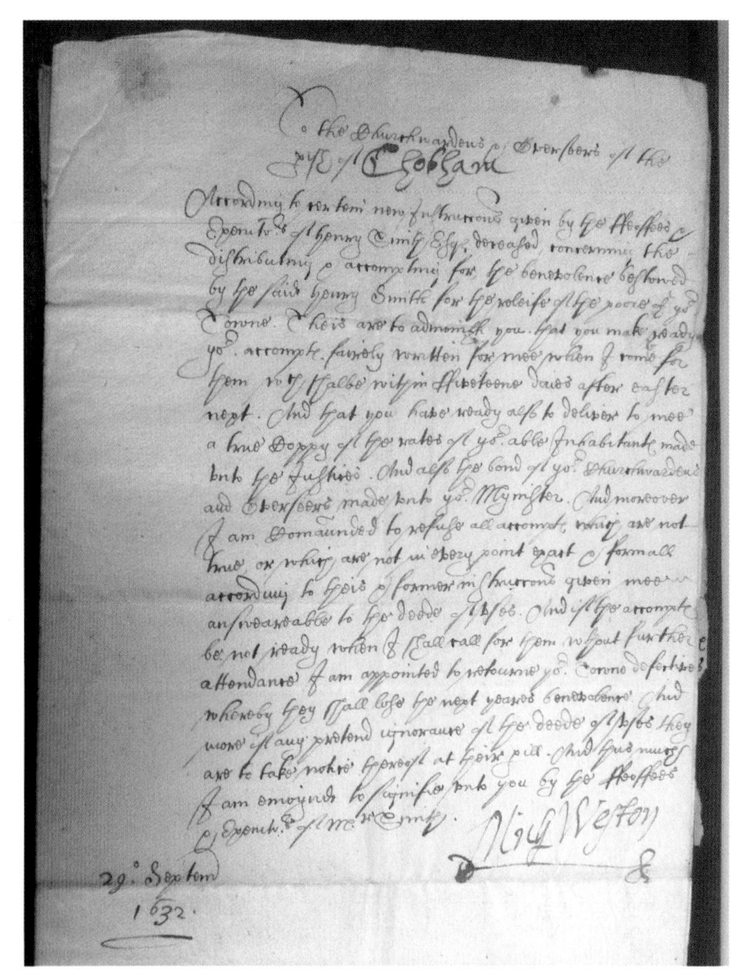

To the Churchwardens & Overseers of the
Towne of Chobham

According to certaine new instructions given by the ffeoffees &
Executors of Henry Smith Esq. deceased concerning the
distributing & accompting for the benevolence bestowed
by the said Henry Smith for the releife of the poore of yor
Towne. These are to admonish you that you make ready
yor accompts fairely written for mee when I come for
them wch shalbe within thirteene daies after easter
next. And that you have ready also to deliver to mee
a true Coppy of the rates of yor able Inhabitants made
unto the Justices. And also the bond of yor Churchwardens
and Overseers made unto yor Minister. And moreover
I am Commaunded to refuse all accompts which are not
true or which are not in every point part & formall
according to theis & former instructions given mee
answearable to the deede of uses. And if the accompts
be not ready when I shall call for them without further
attendance I am appointed to returne yor Towne defectives
whereby they shall lose the next yeares benevolence. And
none of any pretend ignorance of the deede of uses they
are to take notice thereof at their perill. And thus much
I am enjoyned to signifie unto you by the ffeoffees
& Executors of Mr Smith.

Mich Weston

29o Septem
1632.

A letter, dated 1632, from Michael Weston to the overseers of the Surrey parishes bidding them to a meeting at the Star Inn, Kingston. It is a pro-forma, Weston having filled in the town (in this case 'Chobham') in the correct space.

silk weaver and a blacksmith; in the third division, the Clink, a girl was bound out to a widowed bone lace maker. Occasionally money in St Saviour was spent on food: in 1632, the overseers provided victuals to householders who fitted the criteria of special need, 'in sickness, being very poor aged & past labour' and 'having a great Charge of Children'.

The recipients included Edith Cotton, 'a poor aged woman', who received a 'petticoat and a waistcoat with a badge of HS on the breast of the waistcoat' in 1633. She had married Roger Cotton, a Southwark victualler in 1594. He had achieved a modest prosperity. But the Cottons' fortunes declined: Roger ceased to be a ratepayer in 1622 and in the early 1630s he twice petitioned for parish relief, emphasising his lawful, honest past and his current need: 'Your poor petitioner with his aged wife is grown into years whereby their labours are both past that they cannot take pains whereby to relieve themselves'. Edith died in 1634, the year after she received her petticoat and waistcoat, and Roger two years later, by which time he was living in a parish almshouse.

By the early 1630s, instructions from Smith's Charity had been issued 'for the disposing' of his gift to all the parishes. At this stage, we see the appearance of a Michael Weston (perhaps related to Michael Weston, the great Wealden ironmaster of

Cowden and Robertsbridge, whose family had manufactured guns there since the sixteenth century). Weston was appointed by the trustees to ride out into Surrey, where the greatest concentration of the parishes were situated, and ensure that the grants were distributed there according to the regulations and criteria established by Henry's will. If Weston were to find that any parish was 'in default in its performance', then that parish would lose 'one year's receiving of the gift'. One such set of instructions survives for the parish of Send and Ripley.[41]

> Whereas divers great sums of money for the purchase of lands, have been given and conferred by Henry Smith seq. deceased, and since by his feoffees, out of his estate unto the towns and parishes in the county of Surrey, for the due employment whereof his trustees have authorized Michael Weston, gent. from henceforth in their names to repair unto the said several towns and parishes, and there to see that the monies severally given to them be duly disposed and distributed according to Smith's will as declared in his deed of uses.

Weston's activity is seen in the pro-forma letters he issued, ordering parish officers to appear before him at the Star Inn in Kingston. In one that survives, Weston himself has filled in the parish, Chobham, and the date, 2 June. The year is 1632, the first year that another Surrey parish, Mortlake, received money from the charity: when the parish officers, Fraunces Grenowayes and Richard Lee, and the parish overseers, John Poole and Henry Liford, first made out a bond to guarantee their proper administration of the charity, when the terms of Henry's bequest were inscribed in their vestry book and when they first recorded their distribution – again in the form of clothing.

On arrival at the Star Inn, officers no doubt presented their accounts, very possibly the surviving vestry book, in which the terms of Smith's will and the earliest disbursements are neatly written. Mortlake received £3 a year from the charity. The first account is from 1632. The clothing was 'badged' with Henry's initials, according to the requirements laid out in his will: 'A coat with H and S' costing sixteen shillings was given to William Davies, 'aged poor and past labour', who also received a pair of shoes. The churchwardens were also keen to stipulate that the recipients were the poor in need, through age, disability and sickness. John Lidgall, 'aged and lame', received a 'waistcoat', while 'Widow Watson', described as 'a very aged woman and a needy person', also received a waistcoat; Daniel Wingrave, 'being poor and sick', was given a 'jerkin'; and there were waistcoats and 'pairs of shoes' handed out to Widow Eager and Widow Moss, 'being no less poor and aged'.

These were the needy poor of Henry's regulations. Several were also receiving parish relief. The overseers paid Widow Watson a pension of eight pence a week (rising to twelve pence), and a further five shillings in 'regard of her long illness'. Widow Moss was also a weekly pensioner, whilst the parish paid Davies's rent of ten shillings and gave him a further £1 and five shillings over the course of the year.

Three years later, in 1635, the overseers again used the charity to provide clothing, this time recording the materials bought and the cost of making them up: '4 yards of Kersey to make doublet and hose for old Samuell' reads one entry and another tells how another yard made a waistcoat for Goodwife Pate. In contrast to this targeting of clothing to a few, in April 1649 – in the midst of several years of scarcity and high food prices – the parish officers in Mortlake chose to distribute Henry's £3 in the form of sixty twelve penny loaves – perhaps all the labouring families in Mortlake received a loaf that Sunday.

THE RICHMOND COMPLAINT

The death in 1632 of Richard Amherst sparked the first of several lawsuits to be filed against the charity after Henry's death. Amherst had left insufficient funds to cover the repayment of his debt to the charity. His £1,000 debt had been assigned to the town of Richmond by the will, and on 13 February 1653, John Bentley and John Thorpe, overseers of the

'Hamlet and Village of Richmond otherwise called West Shene for and on behalf of the poore people of the said Village', issued a Complaint against Smith's Charity for non-receipt of their money.

The overseers named the prominent Sussex trustees, John Middleton and Amherst, both by now dead, as the two chief culprits in the matter, claiming that the two men did not 'manage the trust in such manner as Smith expected and intended'; it was this situation, they maintained, which had led to the Chancery decision of 1626 which deposited the men's debts at the service of the charity. 'By the deed and will', they wrote, 'the poor of Richmond are entitled to the one thousand pounds.' Since Henry's death it seemed that the churchwardens and overseers of Richmond had been petitioning for the money and had been repeatedly informed that 'there was no doubt or question to be made but that the full sum . . . should be laid out in land for the poor of the town.' They had received, they wrote, a smaller sum of money but the original amount promised in the will had not been forthcoming.

Furthermore, the men of Richmond complained that the only survivor of the original trustees, Richard Lumley, by now Lord Lumley, and Henry Henn, with the connivance of William Rolfe's brother-in-law John Goodwin (tenant of the Warbleton estate among others), had since Henry's death been lining their pockets with the charity's money and had 'much enriched themselves by their breach of the trust'. The charity's trust and the intentions of Henry Smith's will, wrote the complainants, had been 'neglected and broken'. John Goodwin, in particular, they claimed, had been leasing several of the charity's manors and other properties at rents far below their annual value. Furthermore, Goodwin (who was married to the sister of Rolfe's heiress wife, Sarah Deane) was manager of the estate and in that capacity 'together the three have contrived to conceal a great part of Smith's real and personal estate and pretend payment and satisfaction of debts where none was really due or paid. They compound pretended debts at and for small sums of money and in their accounts set down the full sums of the said pretended debts to be satisfied and paid. They set up pretended debts due from Smith unto themselves, when in truth nothing was due to either of them.'*

Amherst's widow, Margaret, was also named in the Richmond Complaint as a co-conspirator in setting up a pretended debt which Henn, Lumley and Goodwin had claimed was due to Amherst from Henry Smith: the courts had awarded Margaret the money – which coincidentally came to almost exactly the £1,000 which Amherst had owed Henry. The complainants asserted that if there had been a debt owed to Amherst, which they doubted, then it should have been paid from the 'overplus' of Henry's personal estate rather than taken from the portion promised to Richmond in his will. Furthermore, they claimed that Amherst had not been insolvent at his death: far from it, he 'died possessed of a large real and personal estate far more than sufficient to pay his debts . . .'

The poor of Richmond, the Complaint went on, had received no interests or profits on their legacy for about seven years, and have not at any time received more than £40 per annum (for the £1,000); sometimes the sum had been less than that, and sometimes they received nothing at all. The complainants therefore claimed £1,300 owing to Richmond (of interest as well as the principal) 'which if the same might be paid in to some of the chief Inhabitants of this said Towne the same might and would be employed to a great Advantage & benefit of the poor of the said Towne, they being very numerous.'

In response to the Complaint, on 4 May 1654, Lumley, Henn and Goodwin protested that as they had none of them acted as executors of Henry Smith's will they could hardly be held accountable

* John Goodwin was from a longstanding Surrey/Sussex border family. He was the Member of Parliament for, respectively, Haslemere, East Grinstead and Bletchingley between 1641 and 1660. The *History of Parliament* reports that he was 'viewed with suspicion' by those who worked with him. He died in 1674 and is buried at Worth, Sussex, the site of another of Smith's estates.

for his personal estate. They went on to say that the complainants could not claim more than the £1,000 debt named in the will. That money was, according to the legacy, to be spent on land and the defendants had not proved to their satisfaction that they were not profit-seeking property holders. They also protested that the now deceased executors ('persons of Quality and Integrity') of Henry's will had done their utmost to recover the debt owed by Amherst and had eventually recovered £800 – which they claimed had been perfectly acceptable at the time to 'divers of the parishioners of said Parish of Richmond', who were 'happily as vigilant and careful of the said poor as the said Complts seem to be'; they also produced an indenture dated 10 December 1641 to back up this statement and prove the consent of the parishioners.

After this agreement had been sealed, in 1633, according to Lumley, Henn and Goodwin, the sum of £40 per annum was paid to, and for the use of, the poor of Richmond 'to be issuing out of the manors of Knowle, Sevenoaks, Kempsing and Seale in Kent (worth £100 above all charges). Ever since the indenture of 1641, these rents and profits have answered to the use of the poor (after tax).'[42] The parish of Richmond received into the twentieth century a yearly grant from the revenues of the estates of Kempsing and Seale.

A view of the Thames at Richmond in 1620, showing the old royal palace. The parishioners of Richmond and the adjoining village of Sheen filed a Complaint against Smith's Charity when they did not receive the money they had been bequeathed.

THE SETTLING OF THE TRUST

The 1630s saw other properties bought and allocated. In October 1635 the trustees bought an estate in Shrewsbury from Thomas and Frances Chlemick for £400 for the benefit of the poor of Shrewsbury; at some point after 1653 it came into the hands of the town's corporation. In 1636, Sir Christopher Nevill sold an estate of 290 acres in Tolleshunt D'Arcy on the Blackwater estuary in Essex to the trustees for £2,800. Nevill had acquired the estate through his wife, one of the five daughters and co-heirs of Thomas Darcy.

The arrangements developed over the 1630s were confirmed by deeds enrolled in Chancery in December 1641 by the surviving trustees (William Rolfe, the Earl of Essex, Lord Lumley, Richard Gurney, Christopher Nevill, Henry Henn, George Whitmore and Henry Jackson). Virtually every parish in Surrey received a bequest, as did a further seventy-five parishes in twenty-one counties. Seven counties had only one parish but in Sussex, where the Sackville influence was so strong, there were thirteen.

How were parishes chosen to receive Henry Smith's charity? As well as the blanket grant to Surrey, there were other parishes scattered over several counties that clearly benefited from direct connections to the trustees. The influence of the Parkhursts can be seen in the grants to Pirford (now Pyrford) and Ripley; Calne in Wiltshire was the constituency of George Lowe; the seat of Sir Christopher Nevill was at Newton St Loe; the birth place of Sir William Blake was Andover; Henry Henn's parish in Winkfield received a grant, as did three parish churches in Chester, where he had once served as a bailiff; Lichfield had connections with both the Earl of Essex and William Wingfield; Lumley's influence can be seen in the six parishes in County Durham: Lumley, Chester-le-Street, Hartlepool, Gateshead, Heseldon and Murton. Lumley's presence also explains several of the Sussex parishes chosen, such as Stoughton and Westbourne, as well as the allocation of £5 a year for maintaining the highway between Harting and Rogate, a grant with absolutely no warrant in Henry's bequest.

About a half of the chosen parishes received £1 to £5 per annum. Less than a tenth of the parishes

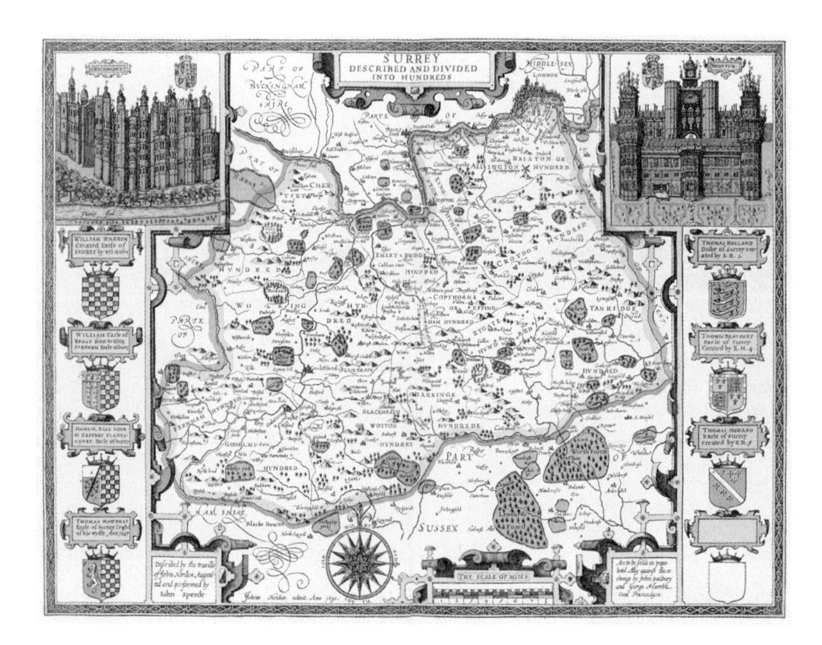

A map of Surrey by John Speed published in 1611–12. In 1641, when the trustees officially apportioned the grants to the parishes, not a single parish in Surrey was left out.

THE FOURTH EARL OF DORSET

The descendants of the third Earl of Dorset struggled with the inheritance of his vast debts. The fourth earl paid further for his association with the king's cause – he suffered heavy fines when the Royalists were defeated. In 1645, the fourth earl had hoped that the dowry brought by his son Richard's marriage to Frances Cranfield, the daughter of the Earl of Middlesex, might enable Richard to buy back Knole; but in 1647, there was still £4,000 remaining of the fine demanded by the Committee of Compounding.

An inventory of a 1645 sale of goods from Knole after the fourth earl's death shows that his descendants flogged off quantities of household goods, from the magnificent (an entire room hung with gilt leather and a 'rich gilt couch bedstead and pillows of green velvet with silk and silver lace') to the rudimentary – Goodwife Marshall from Maidstone purchased 'four old stool pans & a chamber pot of pewter'.

In 1653, Henry Smith's trustees granted Richard, by then fifth earl, an 82-year lease on Knole and the advowsons of Sevenoaks, Knole, Seale and Kempsing – for the sum of £100 per annum. Soon after the Restoration, an Act was passed which settled the Sackville manors of Knole, Seale and Kempsing in Kent, all of which had been mortgaged to Henry Smith, on the Dorsets and their heirs – and they were to take final ownership at the end of their 100-year lease. It was pointed out that the poor of those parishes who were meant to benefit from the rent from the estates received no more than the £100 charged by the trustees; the Act also pointed out that as Knole cost the charity at least £150 a year to maintain and repair, the situation hardly fulfilled the spirit of Henry Smith's bequest.

Edward Sackville, fourth Earl of Dorset (1590–1652) by Sir Anthony Van Dyck, *c.*1638. The famously good-looking Dorset's financial fortunes suffered not only from the extravagance of his brother the third earl, but from the fines exacted by the state as punishment for his association with the Royalist cause.

received over £10 per annum. Pershore in Worcestershire received the largest – £50 per annum. Worcestershire was associated with the Thomas Smith side of Henry's family and Pershore Abbey had long connections with the manor of Longney (from whose rents it derives its grant) but why Pershore should have been apportioned so much more than any other parish remains unclear.

It seems certain that the deeds confirmed and secured arrangements that had already been agreed to. The sums allocated to Lambeth, Mortlake and the Southwark parishes, for example, match the money given to them in the 1630s. Braintree in Essex received £12 a year by the deed: it was one of fourteen parishes funded by the Tolleshunt D'Arcy estate. In 1637, as an eighteenth-century history of the town's benefactions records, Henry Jackson

> at the desire and request of William Lyngwood Gent caused the sum of 12li. to be sent to Braintree with which was bought 6 pieces of Gray Cloth out of which were made 21 Coats for men & 6 Gowns for women & the remaining two yards was given away as was also the coats & gowns upon the 21 day of December following.

The parishes of Terling and Braintree both received their portions from the income of the Tolleshunt D'Arcy estate – both were known for being centres of Puritanism. This suggests that they might have engaged the interest of at least one of the Puritan trustees, notably Henry Jackson: it was quite probable that he secured the money for Braintree, a market town and weaving centre lying five miles to the north of Terling, which in the early seventeenth century suffered from particularly acute social problems owing to a volatile and highly vulnerable textile industry. Like so many towns of comparable size, Braintree received many charitable legacies: there were almshouses, a 'hospital' and a 'pest-house'.

In 1658, the Tolleshunt D'Arcy estate and its dependent parishes (these included Bungay in Suffolk and Fletching in Sussex) broke off from the main body of Smith's Charity and formed a splinter group with their own trustees appointed. It would appear that two years earlier, in 1656, the two surviving trustees, Sir Henry Henn and Sir Richard Lumley, had approached the governors of Christ's Hospital with a view to their taking over the administration of Smith's Charity (as recommended ten years before by Richard Gurney). Both men were old by this time and infirm, but Lumley appears to have been the main driver in proceedings, with Henn less enthusiastic; in fact, the Christ's Hospital records of the case, which was heard before Chancery and continued for two years with 'large debate', suggest that Henn was a troublesome filibusterer, who had to be placated and persuaded at every turn (one alderman was ordered to make the journey to Winkfield to try and win him round).

As it turned out, they need not have bothered, as the governors of Christ's Hospital at length elected not to take up the administration of the charity (the sticking point appearing to be that the old trustees required the new ones to be held responsible for any of their past actions, which suggests that Henn was victorious).

Yet according to the Chancery records, the local trustees of those Essex parishes benefiting from the Tolleshunt D'Arcy estate complained that Henn and Lumley 'who are both very aged and live at a great distance from the said Manors & lands' were 'disabled from managing and discharging the said trust & the poor parishioners are much prejudiced'. They recommended that the old guard should give way to a new board of trustees, drawn up especially for the Essex estate. This was agreed to by Henn and Lumley, and a separate board of trustees comprising Sussex and Essex figures was named in 1657, including Christopher Nevill's grandson George Nevill, Herbert Morley, a leading Parliamentarian in Sussex, Robert and Carew Mildmay, whose family seat was at Terling, and William Lyngwood, a prominent figure in Braintree; in 1669, at Witham in Essex, a new Deed of Charitable Uses was drawn up.

The Tolleshunt branch of Henry Smith's benefaction became from this moment a purely Essex concern run by Essex men. How this arrangement was

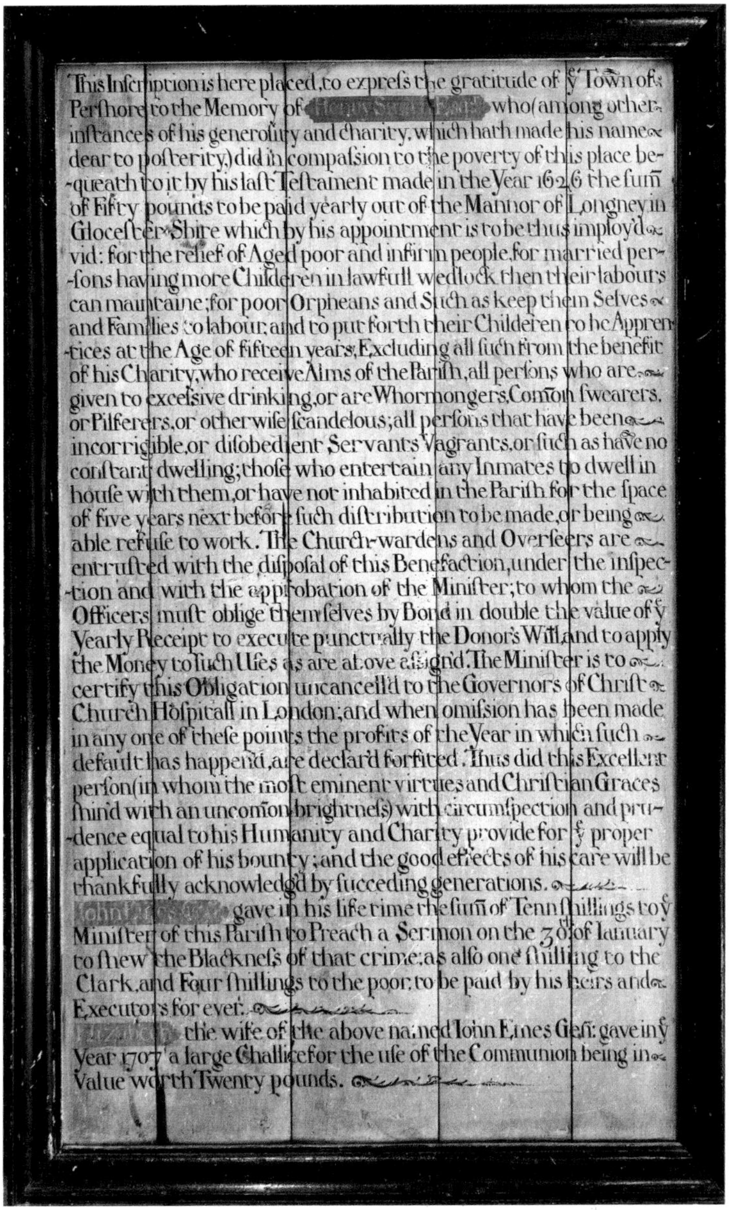

This Inscription is here placed, to express the gratitude of ye Town of
Pershore to the Memory of who (among other
instances of his generosity and charity, which hath made his name
dear to posterity) did in compassion to the poverty of this place be-
-queath to it by his last Testament made in the Year 1626 the sum
of Fifty pounds to be paid yearly out of the Mannor of Longney in
Glocester Shire which by his appointment is to be thus imploy'd
vid: for the relief of Aged poor and infirm people, for married per-
-sons having more Children in lawfull wedlock then their labours
can maintaine; for poor Orpheans and Such as keep them Selves
and Families to labour; and to put forth their Children to be Appren-
-tices at the Age of fifteen years; Excluding all such from the benefit
of his Charity, who receive Alms of the Parish, all persons who are
given to excessive drinking, or are Whormongers, Common swearers,
or Pilferers, or otherwise scandelous; all persons that have been
incorrigible, or disobedient Servants Vagrants, or such as have no
constant dwelling; those who entertain any Inmates to dwell in
house with them, or have not inhabited in the Parish for the space
of five years next before such distribution to be made, or being
able refuse to work. The Church-wardens and Overseers are
entrusted with the disposal of this Benefaction, under the inspec-
-tion and with the approbation of the Minister; to whom the
Officers must oblige themselves by Bond in double the value of ye
Yearly Receipt to execute punctually the Donor's Will, and to apply
the Money to such Uses as are above assign'd. The Minister is to
certify this Obligation uncancell'd to the Governors of Christ
Church Hospitall in London; and when omission has been made
in any one of these points the profits of the Year in which such
default has happen'd, are declar'd forfited. Thus did this Excellent
person (in whom the most eminent virtues and Christian Graces
shin'd with an uncommon brightness) with circumspection and pru-
-dence equal to his Humanity and Charity provide for ye proper
application of his bounty; and the good effects of his care will be
thankfully acknowledg'd by succeeding generations.
gave in his life time the sum of Tenn shillings to ye
Minister of this Parish to Preach a Sermon on the 30th of January
to shew the Blackness of that crime: as also one shilling to the
Clark, and Four shillings to the poor; to be paid by his heirs and
Executors for ever.
the wife of the above named John Ernes Gent: gave in ye
Year 1707 a large Challice for the use of the Communion being in
Value worth Twenty pounds.

Pershore in Worcestershire received an annual grant of £50, and no record survives as to why it was so much larger than that given to the other parishes. This board in Pershore Abbey gives Henry top billing among the list of the parish benefactors and reiterates the instructions regarding administration which he had laid out in his will.

received by Tolleshunt's Sussex and Suffolk parishes is another story – and it takes a century to unfold.

A NEW GENERATION OF TRUSTEES

In an indenture of 1658 there is mention of the last two still remaining of the original trustees: Lord Lumley and the 81-year-old Sir Henry Henn. The estates and properties and their tenants by now belonging to the charity were listed, including the house ('and shops') lately the residence of Henry Jackson in Silver Street. There were lands on Telscombe Down, Sussex (217 acres with rights of 'herbage' or feeding for 495 sheep together with

An agricultural surveyor rides out in 1590. The care of the vast landholdings of Smith's Charity would have fallen to professional men such as this.

feeding for 29 bullocks and 7 horses 'upon the downs and commons of the manor from 1 May to St Andrew's tide' and 29 tons or loads of good and sweet hay per annum). The trustees were to hold all these, it was reported, 'for one whole year at the rent of one peppercorn if it be demanded'.

This indenture witnesseth that Viscount Lumley and [Sir] Henry Henn in conformity with the Commissioners' nomination and appointment, and to the end that the freehold and inheritance of the manors, etc., may be secured, and their rents and profits ordered and supposed for the relief of the poor of the several towns villages and places upon which settlements have been made, and in consideration of 5s. paid by John Lumley et al., have granted John Lumley et al. all the property specified.

TERLING

Terling was an agricultural village, dominated by a small number of farmers. Its agriculture was primarily for the market: it lay close to two market towns – Witham and Braintree – and was six miles from Maldon, a port sending grain down to London.[43] If its yeoman farmers experienced some prosperity, the parish also saw increasing poverty: its population increased by some three-quarters between the early sixteenth and late seventeenth centuries, most of the increase taking place before 1625, and most of it concentrated on the number of labouring poor families. The growing social differentiation was supplemented by a widening cultural gulf in the parish as a group of committed Puritans sought to distance themselves from the customs of their neighbours and to impose a more godly order in the parish. The group that emerged were religious activists – at odds with local custom, with their poorer neighbours and, in the years before the Civil War, with a Church establishment that they regarded as insufficiently Protestant.

As the early seventeenth century progressed, the tempo of prosecutions for offences such as non-attendance at church or drinking on the Sabbath increased and from the mid1610s committed groups of Puritans dominated local office. This Puritan activism brought them into conflict with both state and Church. In 1627 four Terling men refused to pay the Forced Loan, one of Charles I's extra-legal attempts to raise money without Parliament. Terling and its pastors were increasingly at odds with the ecclesiastical authorities that they considered were turning, under William Laud, in too popish a direction. Thomas Weld, the vicar of Terling (1627–32), publicly confronted Laud. His successor, John Stalham, pressed on by his parishioners, defied Laud's injunctions, among them that the communion table should become an altar. As war approached, one Terling Puritan abused an Essex gentleman, an ally of Laud's and a Royalist, as 'a Pope, who kept twenty Popes in his house'.[44]

Although this was in part a social response to perceived problems, the same period seems to have seen attempts made to make it increasingly difficult for poor households to settle in Terling (including in one case the parish forbidding the banns of a poor couple to be read). For the anxious reformers of Terling the alehouse was particularly a haunt of idleness and vice, and a source of disorder and ungodliness. In

The parish church of Terling, Essex. Terling was a centre of Puritan activity and one of the parishes allotted a grant by Smith's Charity, quite possibly at the behest of Henry Jackson or William Rolfe.

1620 the leading parishioners complained that the activities of its alehouse keepers had given Terling an evil reputation: the drunkenness and disorder that they encouraged was 'shameful to be spoken of . . . whereby the name of God is highly dishonoured, idleness maintained and our parish of itself poor enough impoverished and decayed'.

These targets will be very familiar from the discriminations made in Henry Smith's bequests – the drinker, the swearer, the idle and indeed those who had only lived a limited time in the parish. And in the 1630s, the cultural division which isolated the Terling poor as a group to be disciplined and singled out was reinforced by the wearing of badges – a generation before badging became such a widespread and hated humiliation.

Terling's reputation for Puritanism evidently spread beyond its immediate vicinity: Stalham was led there by reports that the villagers were 'a fasting and praying people'. A village like Terling would have had plenty of connections with London through trade and personal links. If one wants to explain how Terling came to be allocated £14 per annum out of Smith's bequest, then the most likely reason is that its reputation – if not more direct links now lost to view – brought it to the notice of a Puritan trustee, perhaps William Rolfe, more probably Henry Jackson. Terling was a village dominated by a Puritan elite that pursued policies echoing the categories of the Smith bequest.

Among the new trustees of 1658, listed in the indenture, were several demonstrating the influence as before of the Surrey connection but also a strong showing from Berkshire, the home county of the Henns. They included Lumley's son John Lumley of Stansted, Sussex (who died within weeks of the enrolment of the deeds) and Henn's nephew, Henry Henn of Chobham, Surrey. The additional new trustees included John Thynne of Egham, MP for Saltash (though recorded as 'taking no part in public affairs' during the 1650s), and the successful lawyer Sir Edward Thurland, the MP for Reigate; John Hercy was another lawyer and a neighbour of Henn's in Berkshire, as was William Pulteney from Bray (whose family also owned twenty-six acres of St James's London). Valentine Pettit was a prosperous textile merchant and member of the Clothworkers: he had been apprenticed to Richard Gurney in 1613 and is listed in 1666 as living in a large house (eight hearths) in Cheapside. He was also involved in a dispute about property in Mayfield, Sussex – which connection may have brought him into contact with the Smith's trustees.

Among the new trustees, John Rushworth is an intriguing inclusion to the list. As well as a lawyer and politician, Rushworth was a well-known historian. By the time he was appointed to Smith's Charity, he had also been for four years the personal secretary to Oliver Cromwell and had that very year been made Registrar of the Court of Admiralty. In 1658, Rushworth was an influential man to have on board.[45]

Also present among the new 1658 trustees were two other figures whose interests may have had a bearing on the fortunes of Smith's Charity: Ambrose Scudamore and Hugh Woodward. Both men were speculative developers in London during the 1650s, apparently working at least some of the time in partnership, with a particular interest in the forty-five acre field in St James's known as Pall Mall Field, which in 1650 contained the tennis court that had been 'for the private use' of King Charles I. At either end of the field there were two fine gardens: one planted with vines and roses and the other with rare plants, roots and herbs, a physic garden. In the middle of the field were five mean wooden outhouses, a pigeon house and a small garden planted with fruit trees.

Detail of a view of London from Southwark, *c.*1630, before the Great Fire, with old St Paul's Cathedral on the left.

In 1651, two years after the execution of Charles I, Hugh Woodward, then a deputy to the Keeper of St James, purchased the field from the trustees for the sale of the late king's lands for £1,842 15s 10d, using his brother-in-law, Ambrose's relation Martin Scudamore, as his agent as he, Hugh, had declared himself 'being formerly a servant to the late King and one that seemingly declared much affection for him'. Woodward became involved with several builders and investors with a view to developing the field – among them Ambrose Scudamore. A ragged fringe of buildings appeared along the southern edge of the field but by 1660 Woodward was dead, having sold part of the field to speculators. The remaining thirty-three acres he left to his trustees to settle his debts.

Scudamore is listed as a tax commissioner in Westminster in 1660 and 1666 and appears in 1671, leasing out land on the southern edge of Pall Mall Field to Robert Rossington, who built a row of houses there.

THE PURCHASE OF THE HALE ESTATE, KENSINGTON

The parish of Kensington, to the west of London, which incorporated the hamlet of Brompton, was known for its rural beauties and 'sweet airs'. Brompton in particular was famed for its market gardens and nurseries that produced salad leaves and green vegetables for the City (eating salad was a French fad which had taken off in seventeenth-century fashionable circles). The first reference to the charity's Kensington estate appears in the indenture of 1653. But it is clear that the trustees had purchased the land at least twenty years before, in fulfilment of the terms of the will that would give the profits from this estate to Henry's poor kindred and for the redemption of captives. Sir William Blake, the vendor of the estate, had died in 1630, so whether the charity purchased the estate directly from him in the months immediately following Henry's death or whether they negotiated with his heirs is unknown.

JOHN RUSHWORTH

The historian John Rushworth, a trustee of the charity in 1658. Engraving by Robert White, 1692.

At the time of his appointment to the trustees of Smith's Charity, John Rushworth was in his mid forties and already heavily in debt. The Rushworths hailed from Northumberland and John was a prominent Parliamentarian (he was a cousin of Sir Thomas Fairfax and also married to the daughter of the Speaker, Sir Thomas Widdrington) and clerk to the House of Commons from 1640. During the meeting of the Long Parliament, Rushworth had developed the habit of taking detailed shorthand notes of all his observations – these formed the basis of his history of the Civil War period. In 1641 he was employed as a messenger between the Commons and Parliamentarian camps in the north.

In 1644 he was Commons' licenser to the press with responsibility for supplying news in the interest of Parliament as well as writing material that promoted the reputation of the New Model Army. Rushworth's *Historical Collections* was published in 1659 and dedicated to Richard Cromwell, son of Oliver. He survived the restoration of the monarchy a year later, despite rumours of his complicity in the execution of Charles I, and was appointed Treasury Solicitor by Charles II. His fortunes did not flourish, however, from the 1660s onwards: despite holding lucrative posts and inheriting a large estate from a cousin, Rushworth was mired in debt and died in the King's Bench debtors prison in Southwark, where he spent the last six years of his life, his mind enfeebled by age and brandy.

Blake had been resident in the village, then in the County of Middlesex, since 1606. Blake was an established figure there. A Justice of the Peace, he had built up a considerable property in Kensington and Brompton, and also along the Thames in Chelsea, Westminster and Knightsbridge. In 1607 he had purchased for £1,100, from Francis Shuckburgh, a farm in Kensington with thirty-two acres called Sandhills, forty-two acres of arable in Eastfield and eleven lots in West Meadow. Blake added to this with two purchases in 1618 from the Earl of Lincoln. One, costing £200, was fourteen acres in Westfield, which lay on the north side of King's Road, and another consisted of five acres and a house on the Fulham Road. All these lands were let on long leases. Blake's next purchases were of a nine-acre meadow in Thamesmead and another thirty acres known as Coleherne in the Earls Court area of Kensington.

Blake himself lived in a substantial newly built mansion, Hale House (known locally as Hell House due to its forbidding appearance), which had been built by the Earl of Argyll in 1612. It was sold by the trustees of Blake's will in 1630 to Sir William Methwold, whose family were to become important figures in Kensington and who gave sixteen acres of land behind the house to found an almshouse for the care of 'six poor and single woman aged fifty, free from vice and of good behaviour'. It was later leased to the Cromwell family, who were prosperous innkeepers, probably not related to the Protector but whose connection with the house has given rise to stories that it was a Roundhead hideout – even that a recess above the fireplace was where Oliver Cromwell hid from Royalist soldiers.

We have no documentary evidence or conveyance relating to the original purchase by Smith's Charity of the Blake estate – except that the land sold comprised eighty-four and a half acres, two roods and twenty-two perches, and cost the sum of £2,000. The farm was let as a whole, on one lease, from the date of purchase until the last single lease expired in 1805. During that time the original rent of £130 per annum rose to only £151 per annum. We can probably assume that William Rolfe was closely involved in drawing up the original purchase, which the sparse evidence we have for the next forty years or so suggests was not entirely straightforward. The first mention of the estate in Kensington belonging to Smith's Charity occurs in 1658 in a deed concerning the appointment of new trustees. It appears that at this time the land was in the manor of Earls Court – but by 1675 it was recorded as completely freehold.

The unsettled period of the Commonwealth that intervened after the purchase may account for the fact that the estate does not appear to have been tenanted until 1664, when it was leased for seventy years by Christopher Blake, Sir William's grandson, for £130 a year, in consideration of his laying out £500 for improvements and in recompense for his releasing his claim to 'several of the lands'. The property consisted of several fields, one substantial house which had been built by a former lessee, Robert Sewell, and about a dozen smaller houses and cottages. By then, the only surviving of the original trustees was Sir Henry Henn, who was 84 years old and a signatory to the lease. Rent was to be paid half yearly in the hall of the Middle Temple at the Feast of the Annunciation and at Michaelmas.

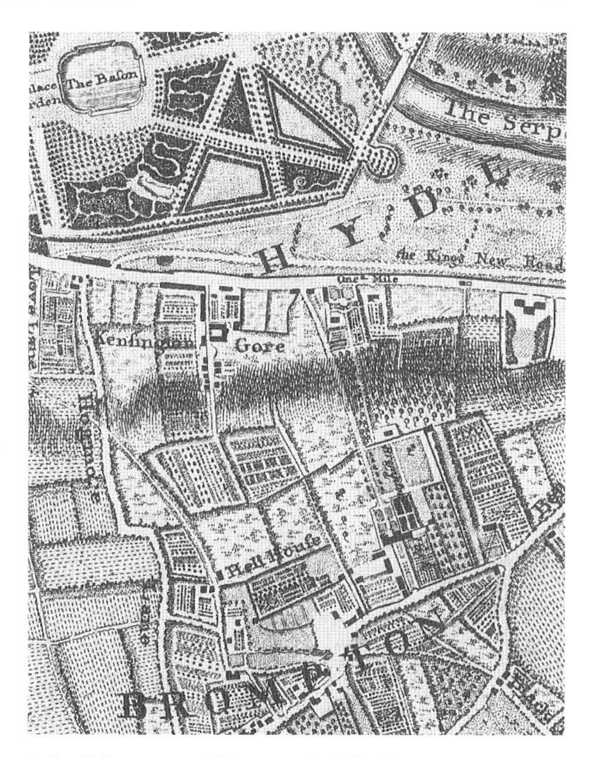

A detail from a map of Brompton by John Roque, 1741–5, showing Hale House as 'Hell House' in the bottom centre.

Seventeenth-century Kensington was still just a remote fringe of the main metropolis – though the parish (comprising the villages of Kensington, Brompton and Earls Court) had become increasingly fashionable as a country retreat for wealthy Londoners such as the Blakes or the Methwolds. The old medieval names of the streets give a flavour of the rural village, its market gardens and agricultural labour: Salad Lane, Hogmire Lane and Thistle Grove. There were flourishing market gardens all along the Thames to the west of London supplying the city with fruit and vegetables. Battersea was renowned for its fine asparagus and Hammersmith for its parsnips. At Brompton Park, where there was a celebrated nursery garden adjoining Hale House, a later observer wrote that a fourteen-acre portion of the Smith's estate was known as 'Flounder's Field' due to its 'moist and muddy state'. This does not seem to have impeded its later development – it is now Brompton Crescent.[46]

The Great Fire of London destroyed the city that Henry Smith would have recognised – including all the houses on Silver Street, and St Olave's Church. English School, seventeenth century.

THE 1660S AND BEYOND

By the 1660s and the restoration of the monarchy, Henry's charity had been running for nearly forty years. An order of 3 February 1663 to appoint more trustees shows how the dramatis personae of the charity had changed. Henn had died in 1660, Lumley a couple of years later and by 1663 the number of trustees had shrunk to only four. These were Henry Henn of Chobham in Surrey, the nephew of old Sir Henry, Sir Richard Bettison, John Goodwin and Sir Edward Thurland,

Nominations were therefore presented that year by the Archbishop of Canterbury and the Lord Chancellor (or Lord Keeper) to make up the number to at least the required thirteen. The accompanying order stressed that additional trustees were required to look after the expanding Surrey estates. The new additions included Sir William Haward, Sir Christopher Wych, Sir Dawes Wymondsold, Arthur Onslow, Roger James, Anthony Thomas, Anthony Bowyer, John Scot, George Evelyn senior, Ambrose Scudamore, John Thynne, Stephen Harvey, Roger Gardiner, Thomas Lee, John Shelbury, Harman Attwood and James Reading. Several well-known Surrey families were included in this list – including the Onslows and the Evelyns.[47]

William Bray, the treasurer of Smith's Charity, writing in 1800, claimed to have discovered a cache of letters from Sir Henry Henn, the second baronet and nephew of Henry's friend and trustee, dated 1674. Where they are now is unclear but, according to Bray, they were addressed from Foljambe Park, Henn's seat in Berkshire. Sir Henry wrote to the clerk of the Smith's trustees, one Mr Byne, to say that he would bring to the next trustee meeting certain papers that he had in his possession concerning the five towns in Surrey. Henn pointed out that as the treasurers of the parishes of Hartlepool, Lichfield and Shrewsbury were all trusted with their documentation, he did not see why the Surrey towns should not be accorded the same privilege. However, months later the correspondence seems to suggest that the papers have been lost: they had been entrusted to his cousin, Henry Henn, who had been nominated a trustee of the charity, and this Henn had gone to Ireland four years before, leaving behind a trunk of papers in his rooms in the Temple which he had instructed be delivered to Mr Byne. They had never arrived.

The grants to the parishes continued to run efficiently. Thirty years after their first recorded grant from Henry Smith, we find the parish overseers of Mortlake, Surrey, were still giving lengths of material (and stays and clasps) rather than clothing to their poor recipients. In 1661, the annual sum from Smith's was paid to 'goodman Thorneton', who made the coats and buttons.[48]

The account of William Gibbon and m^{r} Edwin Browne Church Wardens of the Parish of Mortlake for this present yeare and pd the 24th March 1661[/62] as followeth being the gift of Mr Henry Smith rec of Mr Sawyer the High Constable as by bill appeareth being fifty five shillings sixpence by me William Gibbon.

	li	s	d
Imprimis for 4 yards and halfe of Kersey to make Widdow Ledgall a gowne marked wh H S cost	0	18	0
for makeing the gowne	0	3	0
For stayes and Claspes	0	1	6
More for 4 yards & halfe of Kersey to make goodwife Bonner a gowne cost	0	18	0
For makeing the gowne	0	3	0
For stayes and Claspes	0	1	6
More for 2 yards and halfe of Kersey to make goodman Bonner a Coate cost	0	10	0
For makeing the Coate and buttons	0	2	0
So pd goodman Thorneton as by bill	2	17	0

The charity was still overshadowed by the financial complications of the first trustees. Sir John Pettus, a well-known and somewhat turbulent Royalist and the son-in-law of Sir Richard Gurney, was locked in battle with the Treasury during the 1660s over the debts accrued against Gurney's estate after his death. In 1675, Pettus, aided by Lord Cramond, the husband of Gurney's other daughter, Anne, procured a bill, introduced into the House of Lords by the Bishop of London, that aimed to efficiently 'regulate' Smith's Charity. He claimed that the charity was being badly administered and that its lands 'as have been settled to or for the said charitable uses, have not been managed pursuant to the rules and methods directed by Henry Smith the founder.'[49] Pettus proposed, among other ideas, that a house be purchased that would act as an 'open meeting place' for the trustees who should be renamed 'Masters and Governors of the Charity' and that the estates be settled, for the sake of probity and efficiency, on Christ's Hospital.

SIR JOHN PETTUS

Sir John Pettus was a Fellow of the Royal Society (though an inactive one) and wrote extensively about minerals and mining. He was born in 1613, the son of Sir Augustine Pettus of Norfolk. Like his father-in-law, Pettus was a committed Royalist. He was among those captured by Cromwell's forces at Lowestoft in 1643 and was released a year later. In 1650, he was accused of secretly corresponding with Charles II. For his delinquency he was heavily fined and amassed large debts.

His wife left him in 1657, taking with her many of his valuables – including jewels worth £900. He attributed her delinquency to the fact that she had converted to Roman Catholicism. After a brief reconciliation in 1662, during which he paid her debts of £800, they once more separated and she left, taking quantities of his possessions with her, to enter a nunnery abroad. At her return five years later, Pettus was excommunicated for not paying her alimony of £2 a week. He died in 1685 and was buried in the Temple church.

Sir John Pettus, son-in-law of Sir Richard Gurney, unsuccessfully petitioned the House of Lords for a change in the management of Smith's Charity. Engraving by Robert White, 1683.

The bill was referred to a committee that found in favour of the trustees, pronouncing that they had adequately executed the trust placed in them, and they found no cause to pass the bill. Sir John responded by penning a 'justification' of his actions (Smith's was not the only charity he took to task and there were mutterings that he was wasting parliamentary time by introducing bills which disturbed charities that were running perfectly satisfactorily). In it he claimed to be possessed of 'many evidences, books and writings, relating to Mr Smith's estates', which had come to him through his father-in-law and which he had, in love of his father-in-law, Sir Richard Gurney, 'kept safe through plague, fire and vicissitudes' and that he and Lord Cramond should be given the responsibility of running the charity according to Henry Smith's intentions. He urged transparency, 'that so great a Charitable Gift may not be hid under a bushel but set in a public place (as it deserves) and also managed by Public Persons so that the light and reputation of it, and my clear intents, may be seen by Your Lordships and the Representatives of those towns and counties where they are'.[50]

Pettus was unsuccessful (the Lords appeared to view him as a troublemaker, pointing out that he had a history of attempts to rearrange the governance of various charitable institutions) but it is interesting to note that in the same year a new board of trustees for Smith's, twice as long as the original one, was appointed.

6

The Eighteenth Century

The 1690s had been a difficult decade, marked by economic disruption caused by several bad harvests, by a trade depression and by a steep rise in taxation used to fund wars abroad. Most of the medieval, timbered buildings on Silver Street, including St Olave's and Henry Smith's original house, had been destroyed in the Great Fire of 1666. The charity still owned the site at Silver Street and the new house that had been built upon it (this was later leased to Mr Moore, a silver refiner) but almost all that was left of the neighbourhood that Henry would have known had disappeared.

The income from the Silver Street site was now added to that of the manor at Longney and used to pay for the administration of the charity. There is evidence that the trustees in the 1690s were closely involved with ensuring that the charity was running close to the terms laid out by its founder. It had from the beginning been clear, for example, that the grants to the poor clergy would be made at the discretion of the trustees: in 1698, the vicar of Alfriston, having been awarded an allowance of £5, was suspended after claiming it as a 'right'.[51]

At Warbleton, the charity's landholding in Sussex, the thirty-eight parishes funded by the estate filed a Complaint to the trustees in 1699, complaining that they had not received their portion for the past five years. They claimed fraudulent accounting on the part of Charles Goodwin, who managed the Warbleton estate (and was a descendant of John Goodwin, the dodgy lawyer friend of William Rolfe). Goodwin, as agent of the trustees, was accused of underestimating the income of the estate – the parishes noted several cases of claiming for repairs to tenant farmers and one of claiming over £200 too much in payment of 'king's taxes' from tenants. They also found that he had taken money from Rushlake Furnace in exchange for timber and from Courtlodge Farm for hay – and in neither case had he included the money on the estate accounts. The parishes' representatives pointed out that the value of the woodland at Warbleton 'now ready to be cut' should amount to £200 and they hoped would be put straight to the uses of the charity. Furthermore, they exhorted the trustees to remove their 'agents' (meaning Goodwin and his managers) for incompetence: 'That by the ill management of your agents the Rents are Sunk, & the Inhabitants do inform us they will procure able Tenants that Shall raise the Sum of 100li per annum & Stand to repairs provided you Set aside your Agents.'

The trustees sent Henry Ward of Chertsey and Jeremy Freeland of Cobham down to Sussex to investigate the matter. They found that Goodwin had not only been overcharging his tenants for taxes and repairs but that he was an egregious bully. He had harassed one of his tenants, an 80-year-old man with a bedridden wife, 'by straining for his rent when not paid on very short warning' to such extent that the man's farm had fallen into complete disorder and nobody could be found to take up the lease on it. When the old couple were forced out, they had been unable to afford the repairs that Goodwin demanded of them and the parish had had to step in and pay their costs 'in some way to recover the repute of the farm'. So badly was the estate run that one of Goodwin's tenants, a Charles Bines, had simply refused to pay his rent and met all efforts to extract it from him with 'short and affronting language'.

The Warbleton parishes suggested in their Complaint that their problems might be solved by the appointment of trustees who did not live so far away, asking that the charity

> get the number of Trustees filled up out of Such Gentlemen of Estate as are inhabiting in their Severall Parishes or neighbouring thereunto, have consented together with the 38 Parishes in this Petition humbly to intreat the Same.[52]

The problem of distance in the management of the Tolleshunt estate and the selection of its trustees was also a continuing saga. In 1699, at an inquisition in Chelmsford Town Hall, jurors had been told that the Tolleshunt estate had been leased at too generous a rate to Mr Meriton and Mr Alstone, who earned £228 a year from letting the land and cottages.

Not a penny of this income had been passed on to Tolleshunt's dependent Essex parishes, which were owed seven years' worth of their grants. At a hearing in the Black Boy Inn, Chelmsford, Meriton and Alstone were ordered not only to pay the parishes' legal costs but also to make up their losses: this came to a considerable amount of money (though not the full sums owing): £21 for Braintree, £52 for Tolleshunt, £60 for Henham and £42 for Terling. The Commissioners for Charitable Uses reported that the misapplication of the charity 'is in great measure oweing to the distance and remoteness of the feoffees or trustees . . . from the Lands & Tenements themselves whereby most of them have refused to Act or Concern themselves therein'.

In 1700, a new board of Tolleshunt trustees was appointed under new rules as to their selection. All trustees were to live within a twenty-four-mile radius of Tolleshunt D'Arcy and would have to include the four vicars of the Essex parishes named in the Tolleshunt benefaction. Trustees were henceforth instructed to rent property on leases of no more than twenty-one years and at the best market rent. The trustees were to view the tenants' accounts each year and divide the profits proportionally amongst the parishes according to the shares.

ON THE PARISH

The eighteenth century saw a steep rise in the exercise of and interest in philanthropy in England. The question of the role of public charity in the relief of poverty became a matter of urgent moral debate. In London and other cities a new form of charity developed: the subscription charities that underpinned the creation of new hospitals. Charity and almsgiving was about social order as well as relief of immediate physical and material suffering; it was seen (as Henry Smith had also seen it) as a tool of moral regeneration.

During the late seventeenth and early eighteenth centuries, real wages rose in the wake of increased agricultural and labour productivity and a fairly stable population, and there was a modest rise in living standards. But the experience of poverty remained harsh enough: the dangerous exposure to a bad harvest or trade depression; the uncertainty of work for a family over the course of a year; the dangers to a household of too many mouths to feed; and the inevitable decline into increased poverty with old age. But the period falls into two phases. From the mid eighteeth century, increasingly rapid population increase and declining living standards, the decline of industries in the southern countryside, and enclosure all hit the rural poor.

Throughout the century, parish relief levels rose, despite periodic attempts to cut them back or discourage applicants. Linked to the Poor Laws, from the 1690s the Settlement Laws provided a structure for monitoring the mobility of the poor and the threat they might offer to parish rates and local resources such as common rights. Together with charities such as Henry Smith's, parish relief and settlement could be paradoxical in their implications.

Parish officers would ultimately decide who should receive relief, or the benefit of Henry's gift, but, especially in villages where parish officers and the poor knew each other, refusal might be awkward. As everyone had to have a parish settlement somewhere, by the late eighteenth century, paupers were able to claim for relief in parishes which they had long ago left – indeed, given the increasing complexity of the rules, perhaps had never even seen.

Above all, parish relief was regarded as a right for those poor who had fallen into need. As we shall see, by the mid nineteenth century the Charity Commissioners were to highlight in their reports parishes where the poor regarded Smith's Charity not as a gift but as an entitlement.

Southern counties were increasingly exposed to economic decline and falling agricultural wages. Many of the Smith parishes suffered dire poverty and unemployment. At the end of the century, the period of the Napoleonic Wars brought soaring prices and terrible unemployment. Charles Gwilt, the later chronicler of the charity, recorded in 1825 the results of the conflict: 'The great depression in the value of Mayfield tithes was occasioned by a quantity of land in the parish being thrown out of cultivation.' John Byng, Lord Torrington, in his journal reported taking refuge from a storm in a Sussex cottage in August 1788: 'How wretched do the miseries of a cottage appear! . . . Want of food, want of fuel, want of clothing! Children perishing of an ague! And an unhappy mother unable to attend to, or to relieve their wants, or to assuage their pains; nor to allow time sufficient even for the reparation of their rags; – whilst the worn-down melancholy of her husband (perhaps a shepherd) pinched by cold, and pining with despair, returns at evening close, to a hut devoid of comfort, or the smallest renovation of hope.'

Surrey, where the majority of Smith's grants were distributed, was far removed from the prosperous commuter belt that it was to become a century later. The topographer Arthur Young, travelling through the southern counties of England in 1769, described Surrey as particularly 'backward', blighted

A hedger and ditcher by Thomas Rowlandson (1756–1827). The landless poor suffered most in the agricultural enclosures of the seventeenth and eighteenth centuries.

by its unproductive soil. He observed too that the industrial innovations that were spreading over the rest of the country were less in evidence in the county and that its inhabitants were markedly reluctant to exchange their oxen for horses. Among the commonest rural occupations there were broom-dashing (particularly on the scrubby heathlands), brickmaking and tanning (from which came the associated craft of leather-working or cordwaining). At Walton-on-the-Hill, where a golf course opened in 1904, Young saw only a 'wild and desolate view' and the Surrey landmark of Box Hill he found similarly unpromising, being 'a large, misshapen mass – vast unbroken denseness with little variety'.

When Young was travelling through England, most of the country was still covered by thousands of acres of common land; but it was the beginning too of the great era of enclosures enforced by parliamentary statute, part of a movement to improve agricultural productivity. Enclosure of open fields and common lands had long been a feature of English rural life (indeed, arguably, more land was enclosed in the seventeenth century than in the more notorious eighteenth).

These common lands, where villagers had for centuries collected wood for fuel or building, grazed stock and gathered berries or other foodstuffs, were classified as 'waste' and redesignated for large-scale agricultural purposes. Young was broadly supportive of the agricultural advantages of enclosure but he was also acutely aware of the price paid by poor, landless labourers. He was particularly critical of a system that removed from the poor the means of their own survival, the ownership of a cow, and rendered them instead dependent on the parish for poor relief: 'there is not the least necessity for the evil here complained of, and merely a call that in passing enclosure acts, the rights and interest of the poor should be attended to, which it is too plainly evident they have not been.' In Farnham, Young noted that there were one hundred families who had taken up settlement on the common:

> I examined 47 of them, who possess about 20 acres besides some gardens. 24 of them have 103 children at home, the other families I have not noted. These (147 persons in all) are supported with no other allowance from the parish than £4.8s per week, or 7d a head per week: yet there are only four cows among them. They would readily give up the parish for a cow, and many would agree to repay the cost by instalments. Every 5 persons in the workhouse cost £64 10s 10d per annum; consequently for one year's expense of a family they might establish two on the common free of expense ever after.

The enclosures were to have a profound and disconnecting effect on the life of rural communities, on ideas of communal labour, on thrift and on the value and definition of gainful work: and these in turn would have an effect on poverty and how the responsibility for its relief was viewed and administered. In 1794, it was reported that 8,350 acres of common land in Surrey had disappeared in twenty years.[53] In the archives of the Henry Smith Charity, there survives the Award of Enclosure attached to the Longney estate in Gloucestershire – which took place in 1815. The commissioners were Thomas Fulljames of Gloucester and Richard Hall of Cirencester, acting on behalf of the trustees, led at that time by the Duke of Norfolk and Viscount Middleton. Each tiny parcel of land is numbered and re-allotted – the new configuration of the estate to be read out in the parish church at Longney. The administration of poor relief during this period in the Surrey parish of Shere, one of those that received a benefaction from Henry Smith, is not untypical.

A broom-dasher's hut in Surrey by John Hassell. Surrey was one of the poorest and least agriculturally productive counties in England in the eighteenth century. In the scrubby heathland areas pennies could be earned from selling twig besoms – broom-dashing.

A view of Box Hill in 1733 by George Lambert (1710–65), with Dorking in the distance. Arthur Young failed to see the attractions of Surrey's highest point, describing it as 'a misshapen mass'.

The story of eighteenth-century Shere includes a sudden population growth after 1725: from 550 inhabitants in 1725 to 871 in 1801 and 1,190 in 1831. It was a rural community dependent mainly on keeping sheep and weaving wool, growing flax for linen and rearing cattle for leather tanning. Shere was not an estate village; there were no large landed families on whom the village was dependent for employment. But two old-established families, the Duncombs and the Brays, were leading figures in the parish – the Duncombs were descendants of that George Duncomb of nearby Albury who was one of Henry Smith's original trustees and the Brays had owned at least one of the manors of Shere since 1485.

Poor relief in Shere was administered by volunteer overseers and unpaid officials drawn for their service from among the parish worthies. Relief was paid for by rates collected from those occupying land in the parish – in the legal pattern established by the Elizabethan Poor Laws. The surviving overseers' accounts books from the parish date from 1711 and they show the kind of circumstances and situations that were met with relief. There were some regular pensioners, several elderly widows, some single men and one 'poor maid' for example, who were granted small weekly sums.

Nearly twenty people had their annual rent paid by the parish. Sums were awarded to help with sickness but also to subsidise the carers of the sick and the incomes of villagers who could help in other ways. Thus Widow Bowbrick, who was ill, received eight shillings with two more shillings to pay for someone to tend her. Six shillings was paid for the 'washing of Goody Caplan's clothes' and another small sum to cover the cost of mending the well rope for 'old Blasden'. There was help for unmarried mothers too – four of them in 1776. The parish paid for the costs of dying too: in 1711, the deathbed care, the laying out, the legal expenses, the coffin and shroud, the funeral bread and cheese, and the burial of Widow Kelsey were all subsidised. These duties helped fulfil another prescription of the Poor Laws – that of providing work. In 1719, the Shere vestry book records that they had paid for the flax and its weaving and spinning that went into the cloth that was then distributed by charities such as Henry Smith's.

Shere also had a poorhouse, created during the 1720s in nearby Peaslake by the vicar, George Duncomb. Village poorhouses were a direct response to the Workhouse Act of 1723 that had empowered parishes to build residential buildings for the 'lodging, keeping, maintaining and employing' of the indigent poor.

Henry Smith's Surrey parishes saw many similar poorhouses built in this period: by the Act, those refusing to enter the workhouse were to lose their relief, an attempt to cut back on rising costs. Arthur Young, visiting Worplesden, Surrey, in the 1760s, found an old man and his wife 'living in such a state of wretchedness in a miserable hovel with a small garden on the common as I have not seen any where else; but the love of property keeps them from the parish'. And in Wimbledon, another of Henry's parishes, in 1752 the vestry books record that 'whereas Widow Beakes has been in person and made complaint for relief and desired a pension, which was granted, and a room allowed her in the parish house and by the desire of the parishioners the officers have this day taken an inventory of her goods, but she says she will sooner go a-begging about the country than live in the parish house, it is agreed that she shall not have any relief until she condescends to the order of vestry'.[54]

Many parishes never adopted workhouses and where they were adopted the workhouse may have been small and ramshackle, or in practice turned into something less harsh. But the link made between parish relief and the workhouse had bedded in and was to prove difficult to shift. And the attitude to punishment that the workhouse – especially the barrack-like union workhouses of the nineteenth century – came to represent was to dominate the idea of charitable giving into the early twentieth century.

Walton-on-Thames, another parish which had a Smith's grant, operated on a larger scale: the parish rates paid a contractor £500 a year to maintain the 'poor' in a house of seventy-five inmates. But even in smaller parishes, the rates went towards the livery worn by the overseer of poor relief as well as clothing for the poor. In Wimbledon, in 1750, Richard Lowick, the beadle, had a splendid set of clothes paid for by the parish: '1 greatcoat or "settute" [surtout] coat, blue turned up with red and the cape and sleeves trimmed round with silver lace, a silver laced hat and a pr of buckskin breeches'.

There were many and various attempts by officials to halt the steep spending on poor relief, and the overseers in Walton-on-Thames, in an effort to generate paid employment instead of distributing dole, gave out spinning wheels among the women and children – but it proved unsuccessful. Payment for 'the putting forth of apprentices' that Henry had provided for in his will was another duty of the overseers – and there are records of fines exacted from individuals who refused to take them up when they were offered.

A parish's charitable benefactions supplemented the poor rates – and Shere in 1700 had two such benefactions: Henry Smith's, taken from the income of the estate at Warbleton, gave them £10 a year; and a Mr Maybank had left some land in Cranley (now Cranleigh) which yielded an additional annual fourteen shillings to help provide for Shere's poor. By the end of the eighteenth century, there were four more charitable benefactions, two of them from the Duncomb family, bringing the annual total to £32 9s 2d.

Most of Shere's benefactions were attached to specific activities or requirements – one of them was for teaching children to read, for example, another went to pay for an annual sermon, and another was

This building, dating from the 1720s, was once the poorhouse for the parish of Shere and Peaslake.

used for the buying and giving of bread – but Henry Smith's, true to the prescriptions of the will, left the choosing of the recipients and their needs up to the local trustees, which comprised the rector and churchwardens. In Wimbledon, for example, they every year used Henry's benefaction to pay for great-coats for nominated recipients – usually numbering about six. The parish had several small bequests, like Smith's, which went towards clothing: there are several annual payments for caps, aprons and petticoats for girls and women. The Smith's bequest the overseers evidently decided to give exclusively to men. There is no record of their ages but the names often recur over the years: Joseph English, to take one example, received a new coat approximately every two years between 1743 and 1749.

Shere, as with many other parishes, was fortunate to be able to supplement its rates with charitable endowments. In Hampshire, at the Henry Smith parish of Odiham, they were in receipt of six annual bequests, all dating from the early seventeenth century; they had a poorhouse, almshouses and paid overseers. But not far away, in Broughton, near Andover, the Henry Smith endowment was the only benefaction they received: an annual payment of £5, which the Reverend Samuel Eyre reported was to support 'such inhabitants of this place who are not upon the parish book and have more children begotten in lawful wedlock than they can maintain by their labour'.

DEVOLVING POWER

By the last years of the seventeenth century and the early years of the eighteenth, the property holdings of Smith's Charity, having survived its early vicissitudes, expanded considerably. The five towns had most of them purchased land with their endowment in Henry's will. Croydon, for example, had purchased from Sir Richard Gurney, 'divers meadows and pastures' in Deptford, then on the edge of London: the trustees kept control of it until 1712, when it was made over to the management of the mayor's office of Croydon.

In Kingston upon Thames, the churchwardens used their endowment 'for the maintenance and setting on work of the poor of the said town and for the education and bringing up of poor people in some good Christian course and trade in life'.[55] In Reigate, contrary to the explicit spirit of the 1626 deed, the town leaders set up a school.

Sometimes, however, the devolution of power proved hard to manage. Guildford, one of the five towns that had received £1,000 by Henry's gift, had also been allotted the income from the rents of the manor of Poyle, near the town, with mills, meadows and several properties adjoining the River Wey. It was purchased by the trustees from Sir George Whitmore, and was to provide for the poor of Guildford – with the understanding that any ensuing disagreements were to be referred to Smith's trustees.

In 1703, the mayor of Guildford and others of the town complained to the Attorney General that the Smith's trustee John Wight had in the late 1680s conveyed the lease of the Poyle property to Richard Onslow, another trustee and member of one of the most prominent Surrey families, in what the complainants regarded as an underhand manner and without the approval of the town's overseers. It took three years before the case was heard, in 1706, and Wight was found to have behaved properly: it was, said the court, unnecessary for the trustees to have to account to the mayor for their management of the leases.[57]

In 1704, the Attorney General sued Benjamin Bonwick, representing Smith's Charity, on behalf of the residents, churchwardens and overseers of Reigate for mismanagement. Their complaint focused around a farm in Sussex of forty acres, known as Gardiner's, which had been purchased with the town's £1,000 'some short time' after the death of Henry Smith. Of the trustees who had overseen these purchases (including Edward Thurland, lately the MP for Reigate and son of the 1658 trustee), there was only one survivor: Benjamin Bonwick, now over 70 years old, who had taken the lease on Gardiner's for himself. Several of the deeds relating to the purchase and title of the estate, accused the complainants, 'are conceived to be casually lost or mislaid'. Although the town had been using the rents from the farm for the benefit of the poor 'for fifty years and upwards', the Reigate men were concerned that the possession of the lease was out of their control and that 'inconveniences might ensue'. Bonwick, as it turned out, had refused to transfer his trust or execute any deed that might require him to do so, unless he was required by Chancery decree.

In his reply, Bonwick said he knew it to be true that the property had been purchased by Smith's money but that 'when, by whom, in whose names', he had no idea. He had never, he said, seen any deeds or conveyance but he knew that Sir Edward Thurland had been a trustee of Smith's and said that he had been persuaded by Thurland to join with him in taking Gardiner's Farm – on which he had spent a great deal of money building barns, repairing the premises and felling and selling timber in order to lease the farm to John Greenfeild for twenty-one years at a good price. He had never made any claim to the estate other than in trust for the charity.

The action was evidently intended to ease the smooth creation of a new group of trustees whilst indemnifying Bonwick against any possible charges which might be laid against him for his conduct as a trustee. Bonwick urged a further point. There were two sets of overseers for Reigate: for the Town and the Foreign, the latter that part of the parish which lay within the parish but outside the borough. The charity money was distributed proportionately between the two, and Bonwick requested that this should be continued and that the proportion be mirrored in the composition of the trustees that Chancery should appoint.

MOVING WITH THE TIMES

Throughout the last years of the seventeenth century, the threat to British mariners of being kidnapped and taken into slavery by Barbary pirates had receded. In 1719, Daniel Defoe published his novel *Robinson Crusoe*, in which his eponymous hero is sold into slavery in Salley by corsairs – but Defoe had set the plot of the book seventy-five years before, when the fear of attack by Moorish pirates was much more real. The last call for the redemption of captives

SIR EDWARD THURLAND

Sir Edward Thurland plays a major part in the history of the Reigate bequest. Sir George Whitmore had written to Sir Edward, who became a judge in the Exchequer in 1665 and was known for his incorruptibility, to chastise him for his laxity (on what grounds we do not know) when it came to carrying out one of Henry's trusts for Reigate – and as Whitmore died in 1654, Thurland must have been appointed a trustee well before then.[56] In 1675, Thurland was a local trustee for Smith's trust in Reigate, when it donated £150 for the establishment of a school for the poor, a free school. An acre of land with a house on it was bought for this purpose and conveyed to Thurland as trustee; the vicar of St Mary's, Reigate, the Revd John Williamson, was appointed to run the school. Two years later, it was alleged that Thurland's son Edward had violently ejected Mr Williamson from the school on the grounds that he was a person of 'ill life' and the Thurlands questioned whether the majority of the parish had elected him. They lost the case and Mr Williamson was returned to his post – from then on it was made clear that it was the churchwardens who would be in charge of appointing the headmaster. The link with the Henry Smith Charity was maintained until the nineteenth century, when the school became Reigate Grammar.

received by Smith's Charity had been in 1723 and at least ten years before that the trustees had started investing the captives' money in New South Sea Annuities. With hindsight this would seem to have been a risky venture – and history does not relate whether the Smith's Charity trustees were stung by the notorious South Sea Bubble of 1720; but by 1772, they had successfully applied to Parliament to redirect the captives' money (after waiting for one year for any application to be made for redemption) towards the other recipients of the increasingly lucrative Kensington estate – the poor kindred.

The eighteenth century also saw the end of the protracted efforts of the Sackvilles, descendants of Henry's nemesis, the third Earl of Dorset, to reclaim Knole Park and its surrounding estate. The Sackvilles took back their ownership of Knole House during this period. The Dorsets, since 1724 possessors of a dukedom, were keen to establish that Knole, one of the famed houses of Kent, described by Lord Torrington on his travels as 'having an awful collegiate magnificence', was absolutely theirs.

In 1724, the first Duke of Dorset proposed to give Smith's Charity large tracts of land in Sussex in exchange for full possession of the manors of Knole Park, and the adjacent manors of Kempsing

A prospect of Guildford by Samuel and Nathaniel Buck, 1738, showing the parish church on the top of the hill and the castle to the east of it.

and Seale. The land offered in the Sackvilles' part of the deal was found by the trustees to be of inferior quality but they were nonetheless keen to relinquish the responsibility for Knole: for one thing, it was extremely expensive to maintain. In 1727, they agreed to release sixteen acres of land at Knole in exchange for land owned by the Sackvilles in Headington, Oxfordshire.

But it was to take another thirty years after their lease on Knole expired for the Dorsets fully to reclaim the house and park from Smith's; the trustees finally agreed to relinquish Knole in return for land in Sussex that had once belonged to Lord Amherst – a descendant of Henry's long-suffering friend and lawyer Richard Amherst of Lewes.

In 1791, John Frederick, the third Duke of Dorset, finally settled the matter by Act of Parliament and Smith's Charity released Knole to the Sackvilles via an agreement that had been staggered from 1770. The duke agreed to exchange for Knole a 176-acre farm and two cottages in Reigate, and annual payments owed to the duke amounting to around £60 a year from Mount Bures in Essex (they already had the rents from Headington). The Smith's trustees held on to the manors of Kempsing and Seale for the purposes of the charity and the following parcels of land and property:

The manor house in Sevenoaks (£31. 10s p .a.)

Tenements in Sevenoaks (£4; £2. 10s)

Market house and market tolls in Sevenoaks (£4)

5 buildings or sheds in Sevenoaks (£4. 15s.)

Tenement on Sevenoaks Common (£2. 15s.)

Untenanted tenement near Sevenoaks Turnpike

Garden and field (3½ acres) near Sevenoaks (£14)

Manor and field in Sevenoaks: 2 acres (£8); 3 acres (occupation of John Austin: £10); 6 acres, now in occupation and tenure of Dorset (£24)

Redlands (17 acres in Sevenoaks, Kempsing and Seale parishes, £9)

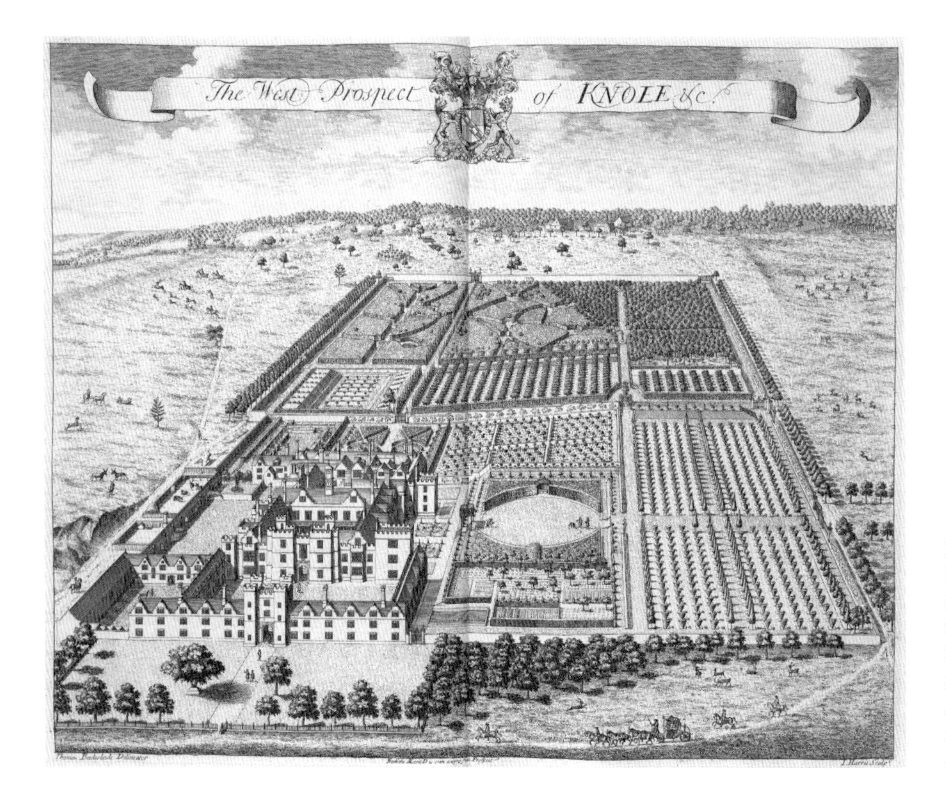

Knole House, which had been leased by Smith's Charity to the Sackvilles for a hundred years, had been further expanded and was now considered one of the glories of Kent. Engraving by Kip, c.1750.

THE LEGEND OF 'DOG SMITH'

The legend of the Lambeth Pedlar, depicted here in an engaving of a stained-glass window in Lambeth parish church, may have been one of the sources for the story of 'Dog Smith'.

In the few mentions of Henry Smith by eighteenth-century historians, he is often confused with a legendary folk figure called 'Dog Smith', whose story seems to have supplied an explanation for so many Surrey parishes being the chief beneficiaries of Henry's will. In the common version of the tale, Dog Smith wanders the villages of Surrey dressed as a beggar and accompanied by his dog: those parishes that treat him well are remembered in his will and those where he is treated badly (the villagers of Mitcham – or in some accounts, Leatherhead – were said to have whipped his dog) were struck off the list. Another version of the story has Smith collecting bones for his dog from his host's dinner tables. John Evelyn mentioned 'Dog Smith, the benefactor of Surrey' in his diaries; and a 'Dog Smith' was among those listed, scathingly, in the republican writer Algernon Sidney's 1698 *Discourses Concerning Government* as one who had made a large fortune through government contracts: 'Old Audley, Dog Smith, Bp. Duppa, Brownlow, Child, Dashwood, Fox, &c . . .'

By the early eighteenth century, however, the myth of 'Dog Smith' or, sometimes 'Beggar Smith', had taken root around the life of Henry Smith the philanthropist. The Complaint made in 1699 to the trustees by the Warbleton parishes refers to Henry as 'Called to this day Dog Smith'. By 1762, when Emmanuel Bowen drew up his map of Surrey, the Dog Smith legend was reproduced on the manuscript.

William Bray, the antiquarian, dated the story of Dog Smith to a century earlier than the life of Henry Smith, speculating that it arose from a confusion with the 'Lambeth Pedlar', who in 1505 was said to have left in his will an acre of land (known as 'Pedlar's Acre, just by Westminster Bridge') to the parish of Lambeth in exchange for leave to bury his dog in the churchyard. His image is preserved in stained glass in the south-east window in the church. This story may also, regrettably, be without foundation – in 1913, a trustee of the Pedlar's Charity said that it was 'all rubbish' and that the land was bequeathed in 1400 by Sir William le Pedlar, the rector of Streatham.

Whatever the truth of these stories of vagrant benefactors, the legend of Dog Smith continues to attach itself to the life of Henry Smith – a legend too picturesque perhaps to be dispensed with altogether.

Windmill built on land enclosed from Sevenoaks waste (£2. 15s.)

4 acres enclosed from Sevenoaks waste (£1. 1s.)

A barn built near the cricketing ground at Sevenoaks on land enclosed from the waste (15s.)

1 acre, parishes of Kempsing and Seal (18s.)

A chalk pit, 21 acres, Kempsing and/or Seal (£8)

Cowlards (now in the tenure of William Austen, £42); and 17 acres enclosed from waste of Sevenoaks and Knowle and now in occupation of Lord Amherst or his tenants

KENSINGTON

Christopher Blake, grandson of William Blake, had taken the lease of the Kensington property from the Smith's trustees. He died in 1672. By his will his leasehold lands passed first to his sister Maria Dorney and then to her son, John Harris. The latter assigned the lease to Richard Calloway of Knightsbridge, an innkeeper, and at the time of its expiry in 1734 the leaseholder was Francis Calloway, Richard's son. Kensington and Brompton were still at this time primarily rural villages but they had benefited from their proximity to the city of London and several large villas had been built there.

Brompton was still renowned for its nurseries, in particular the Brompton Park nursery owned by the celebrated horticulturalist and garden designer Henry Wise, who died in 1734. According to Thomas Faulkner, writing his *History of Kensington* in 1820, one of the large nursery gardens still in Brompton at that time had been in the same family for 130 years. John Strype, whose huge 1720 survey of London and Westminster updated John Stow's of a century and a half earlier, observed that the Penny Post (introduced in 1680) had effected great improvements in communications between the city and its outlying villages: 'The Convenience of this Penny Post is great, with respect to all such as dwell in so many Towns and various Places, as are within ten Miles of the City; who may have Letters to them, and from them, sent every Day in the Week.'

The tenants of the Kensington estate paid the same rent per annum that had been fixed for Christopher Blake – until, that is, 1735, when it was raised from £130 to £250. This was understandably something of a shock to Francis Calloway, then the tenant, who complained to the trustees – who then reduced the sum to £200. In 1749, Calloway sold his interest in the Smith lease to a Dr William Bucknall. The new lessee had made his home at Brompton Hall, a substantial property situated almost exactly on the spot where South Kensington underground station now stands and just outside the boundary of the Smith estate.

Dr Bucknall turned out to be an unreliable tenant and by 1759 he was £800 behind with his rent. In return for repayment the trustees were forced to do a deal by which they cancelled Dr Bucknall's lease and issued a new one to his son, Samuel, at a reduced rate of £151 a year. William Bucknall died in 1763 and Samuel in 1770; Samuel's two sisters then took over the lease of the Smith estate. When they in turn died, their husbands, the Revd Joseph Griffiths and Morgan Rice, moved into Brompton Hall and took over the lease themselves.

The trustees were initially slow to capitalise on a 1772 Act that they had particularly secured in Parliament that enabled them to grant building

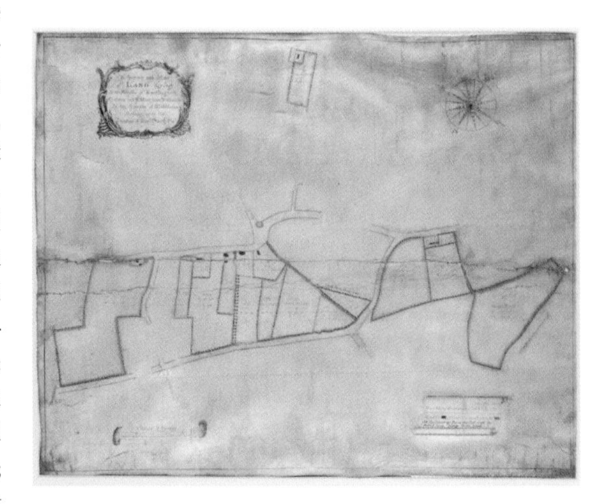

This is the earliest known map of the Smith Charity's Kensington estate. It dates from 1753, before its development and when most of the land was leased to market gardeners.

leases. The heirs of Dr Bucknall were quicker off the mark – inspired presumably by a lucrative flurry of speculative development north of the Brompton Road during the 1760s.

In 1785, Joseph Griffiths sold subleases of pockets of land in Brompton to a Polish architect and theatrical scene painter called Michael Novosielski, who was to prove the most influential and colourful early figure in the development of modern Kensington. A bold and rackety opportunist, Novosielski is best known now for his startlingly grandiose designs for the King's Theatre, Haymarket. Despite being shoddily and hastily put together, Novosielski's theatre, which was larger than any in Europe, was hailed at its opening in 1791 (when Haydn played the harpsichord) as a marvel – even though its architect had had constant run-ins with the Haymarket trustees because of his excessive expense claims and his enthusiasm for putting members of his family on the payroll (his wife was employed as a 'candle superintendent' at £150 per annum).[58]

Michael Novosielski in 1791 by Angelica Kauffmann; he is holding his designs for the King's Theatre, Haymarket.

Novosielski was at the peak of his career when he purchased his two Kensington subleases from Griffiths: both ran for 45 years. These gave him a total of '14 acres 24 p[erches]' at £140 per annum. The leases granted him a patch of land at the top of what is now Brompton Road (it was then a continuation of the old turnpike road leading from Knightsbridge to Brompton and Fulham). Into this muddy and waterlogged portion, known locally as 'Bell field otherwise Flounders', Novosielski squeezed his ambitious development of seventy-seven houses (built to his own designs and two of them named after him) on three separate developments: Michael's Place, Michael's Grove, and Brompton Crescent.

The houses were substantial but designed with the rising urban middle class in mind: three or four storeys in height with iron railings and gardens in front and at the back. In 1792, the famous singer Elizabeth Billington moved into number 16 and William Cobbett, the radical journalist, took up residence in number 11 from 1820 to 1821 – indications that the area had already begun to attract a literary, theatrical crowd. Novosielski also created for himself and his family a house called Brompton Grange that stood nearby, surrounded by expansive gardens.

Novosielski died in Ramsgate in 1795, still only in his forties, leaving half-completed building projects in Piccadilly and in Sidmouth, Devon. But his Kensington estate development was not yet sufficiently profitable to keep his descendants housed at Brompton Grange. For a period after Novosielski's death, the house was taken by the celebrated operatic tenor John Braham – but for the next four decades, the house stood most of the time empty except for a caretaker, until it was demolished in 1845 (and built over by what is now Egerton Terrace).

It took some time for the trustees of Smith's Charity to take action against Dr Bucknall's sons-in-law for exploiting his head lease. As well as Novosielski, Griffiths and Rice had subleased two

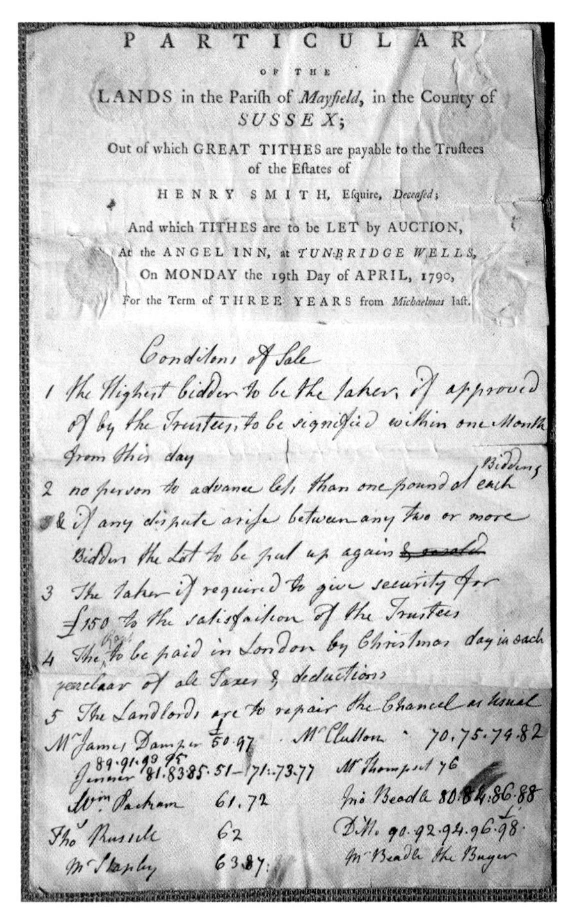

PARTICULAR
OF THE
LANDS in the Pariſh of *Mayfield*, in the County of
SUSSEX;
Out of which GREAT TITHES are payable to the Truſtees
of the Eſtates of
HENRY SMITH, Eſquire, *Deceaſed*;
And which TITHES are to be LET by AUCTION,
At the ANGEL INN, at *TUNBRIDGE WELLS*,
On MONDAY the 19th Day of APRIL, 1790,
For the Term of THREE YEARS from *Michaelmas* laſt.

Conditions of Sale
1 the Highest bidder to be the taker, if approved of by the Trustees, to be signified within one Month from this day
2 no person to advance less than one pound at each Bidding
& if any dispute arise between any two or more Bidders the Lot to be put up again ~~& resold~~
3 The taker if required to give security for £150 to the satisfaction of the Trustees
4 The Rent to be paid in London by Christmas day in each year clear of all Taxes & deductions
5 The Landlords are to repair the Chancel as usual

Mr James Damper £50.97 · Mr Clutton · 70.75.79.82
Jenner 89.91.93 95 81.8385.51–71..73.77 · Mr Thompson 76
Wm Packham 61.72 · Jno Beadle 80.84.86.88
Thos Russell 62 · D.M. 90.92.94.96.98.
Mr Stapley 63.87: · Mr Beadle the Buyer

The revenue from the Mayfield and Alfriston estates in Sussex went into the fund for poor clergy. This particular concerning parish tithes from 1782 is signed by William Clutton.

acres to a Mr Bevan in 1791 and a number of other individuals on which to build their own houses. But it was the sudden rise in building by Novosielski that brought the matter to the trustees' notice – though it was not until 1806 that they applied to the Court of Chancery to have the head lease returned to them: on the grounds that the rent paid for it was inadequate and its term too long. The tenants were called to account for not paying Smith's a percentage of their profits. When they finally repaid their debts, the trustees reported that they were able to invest £1,470 in government securities.

STREAMLINING

This period sees the Smith's Charity beginning to resemble a large-scale operation in the modern sense, employing a range of advisers and consultants with different areas of expertise. By the end of the eighteenth century, the development of the South Kensington estate meant that it was more efficient to split the management of the London properties from the rural estates. The charity's South Kensington estate funds were banked, for example, with Barclay's Bank, founded in 1690.

There is no record as to when Smith's Charity became involved with Barclays but a reference to John Tritton in an undated correspondence suggests that it must have been at least as early as 1785, when Tritton became a partner at the bank. The trustees appear to have met regularly, as required by the will. Most of them were still representatives of Surrey and Sussex landed families: the Onslows, for instance, or the Burrells, the Jolliffes and the Wintertons. The dinners they consumed at various inns when on Henry Smith business were meticulously noted down – and, in 1796, 'a coach with box to Dorking'.

At this time two men entered the employment of Smith's who were to have a profound effect on the future of the charity – and whose descendants were to remain with Smith's for nearly 250 years.

WILLIAM BRAY

The first published account we have of the life and pedigree of Henry Smith and his legacy comes from William Bray, antiquary, solicitor and, for nearly half a century, treasurer of Smith's Charity. In many cases, so many early documents having been destroyed, his investigations, published in 1800, are now all we have of the early workings of the charity. Bray's *Collections Relating to Henry Smith, Esq., some time Alderman of London* includes detailed topographical studies of the landholdings and estates owned by the charity.

The antiquarian and lawyer William Bray was the treasurer of Smith's Charity for many years and the chronicler of its history. His firm and its descendants looked after the charity's affairs for nearly 250 years. Portrait by William Linnell (1826–1906).

Bray was born in 1735, in the village of Shere, Surrey, where his grandfather George Duncomb was the rector. Bray was articled to an attorney in Guildford and in 1757 was sworn in as an attorney of the King's Bench. In 1761, he became clerk of the board of green cloth through the patronage of John Evelyn of Wotton. As well as this, he founded a thriving legal practice in Great Russell Street, London, where he made a speciality of acting for the many families and charities of Surrey. Bray's legal firm took over the administration of Smith's Charity and in 1769 he was appointed treasurer – in which post he stayed for fifty years. Bray's firm, which became Bray and Warren, was to act for the charity for very nearly the next 250 years (and their descendants at the law firm, which still exists, still maintain a connection with the Henry Smith Charity). Bray said himself that 'from an early part of his life he had attended to the History of his Native soil', and the history, topography and pedigrees of Surrey and Sussex were his passion. As an avid antiquarian Bray was in 1772 elected a fellow of the Society of Antiquaries. Tightly bound into the Surrey rural world into which so many of Henry's benefactions had been made, Bray published countless articles and essays and many books – including a five-volume transcription of the diaries of John Evelyn and his completion of his fellow antiquarian Owen Manning's *History and Antiquities of Surrey*. William Bray died in 1832, aged 96, at home in Shere. There is a memorial to him in the parish church – and one of the village pubs is still called the William Bray.

WILLIAM CLUTTON

A surveyor from Sussex, William Clutton was appointed surveyor of the Smith's Charity estates in

William Clutton became surveyor of the Smith estates in 1769, the first of many generations of Cluttons to be closely involved with the charity.

1769, the same year that William Bray took over their legal affairs. The appointment was something of a coup for Clutton – he was then 29 years old and had only been in business as a land surveyor for four years.

William Clutton was born in 1740, the son of the Revd Ralph Clutton, who had migrated from Cheshire to Horsted Keynes in Sussex in the early years of the eighteenth century and was the rector there. The earliest mentions of William describe him as a farmer and agricultural valuer. He first surfaces in practice as a surveyor on his appointment to the job for Smith's estates, having taken over the surveying practice of his father-in-law, Robert Chatfield, who had been the surveyor for the charity for several years. William Clutton's land agency business, underpinned by his work for Smith's Charity, prospered and he conducted it from his house, Ockenden Hall, at Cuckfield, which he leased from the Burrell family. He also acted privately for the families of a number of the Smith's trustees – the Burrells, the Wintertons and the Jolliffes, all of whose descendants were to continue as trustees for the charity.

As the company grew, so did his family: William married twice and had ten children. An anonymous pen portrait of William Clutton, published to commemorate the Cluttons' bicentenary in 1965, adds a not quite explained coda to William's life, suggesting that his many energies in the end overtook him: 'In his anxiety to bring [his children] up properly he ran his business with inadequate assistance and got his accounts into a fearful tangle, which were only straightened out as the result of unremitting efforts by his son Robert, where it was found, contrary to general expectation, that he was owed considerable sums of money in every case.'

It was his son William Clutton Jr, however, who took over the running of the surveying business. He moved with his family to Hartswood House near Horsham, which his father had purchased from one of his clients, and this was to be the Clutton family home for the next hundred years. It was this William's grandson John who was to help shape the future of the South Kensington estate into a new century.

An early map of the Mayfield properties dated 1789 (detail).

7

The Nineteenth Century

In April 1796, a note in the trustees' accounts recorded that 'Mr Geo Gwilt was paid £3.10 – with allowance and "extra" for his work in overseeing' the Kensington estate for a month. There were two George Gwilts at this period to whom this might have applied – the elder a distinguished architect, the younger soon to be an architect as distinguished. It was probably, however, George Gwilt the younger, at this stage only 21 years old and twenty years later to be well known for his remodelling of the tower and choir of St Saviour, Southwark.

The architect Joseph Gwilt completed, and in 1836 published, his son Charles's book on Henry Smith's pedigree and the birth of his charity. Portrait by Robert Anderson, 1810.

THE GWILTS

The Gwilt family, ranging over more than four generations, were to play an important part in the chronicles of Smith's Charity in the nineteenth century. Antiquarians, architects, genealogists and heraldry bibbers, the Gwilt-authored *Notices Relating to Thomas Smith of Campden and to Henry Smith Sometime Alderman of London* provides a sequel to William Bray's collections and fills in many of the gaps. Its author was Charles Perkins Gwilt, a first cousin of George, whose diaries, now in the Bodleian, are covered with pencil sketches of tombs and coats of arms and neat notes of family trees showing the extent of his detailed foraging into the pedigree of the Smiths.

Charles Perkins Gwilt was frail in health, his enthusiasm for research in part a result of being housebound for long periods: he died in 1835, just before his twenty-seventh birthday, leaving *Notices* unfinished. His name is among those of former pupils carved on the gateway known as the Burlington Arch at Westminster School. His father, Joseph, then took up the task of editing the book and adding appendices, including material from the Charity Commissioners' reports on Smith's Charity. Twenty five copies of *Notices* were published in 1836, with Joseph Gwilt's additions. A prodigiously energetic polymath, Joseph Gwilt was by trade an architect, like his father and grandfather, and like them based mainly in south-east London, where he established a successful practice. He was also a sought-after designer of funerary monuments and a Fellow of both the Society of Antiquaries and the Royal Astronomical Society and in 1805 he was appointed surveyor to the commissioner of sewers in Surrey and Kent. On top of all that Gwilt was a prolific writer whose *The Encyclopaedia of Architecture, Historical, Theoretical and Practical* (1842) was a bestseller.

The Gwilts were also kindred, claiming a direct descent from Joan Jackson. This could explain something of their enthusiasm for digging out evidence that placed the Wandsworth Smiths among the more illustrious Gloucestershire Smiths. Joseph Gwilt recollected that in 1826 the Smith's treasurer Reginald Bray, son of William Bray, had shown him the first entry of a Gwilt in the poor kindred account books – the name Elizabeth Gwilt had appeared there as early as 1677.

There is evidence of some competitive antiquarianism between the Brays and the Gwilts. In the margins of an original edition of Bray's *Collections*, now in the Society of Antiquaries library, Joseph Gwilt has pencilled rude remarks. He noted for example that a couple of mistakes in the Latin transcription of the Wandsworth memorial were 'A proof of Mr Bray's ignorance of Latin'. The Gwilts' determination to prove that Henry Smith was related to Thomas Smith seems at least in part to stem from Bray's scepticism about that connection.

More importantly, however, Charles Gwilt had been strongly of the opinion that it had not been the first intention of Henry Smith to restrict the funds for the kindred to those who were poor but rather to those who needed money. The Gwilts particularly objected to the claimants being judged by the trustees on their behaviour to determine the strength of their case. This was a point of animosity with William Bray, who, as treasurer of Smith's Charity, had overseen the distribution of funds. In Bray's *Collections*, he had taken pains to point out that when asked to make clear his definitions, Henry Smith had used the word 'poorest' to describe those of his sister's descendants he had anticipated being in need.

In 1700, there were only four claimants from the poor kindred. By the mid nineteenth century the numbers registering as kindred were rising steeply and so was the income from the Kensington estate.

Since the 1772 act which passed the captives' fund to the kindred, Gwilt noted that claimants had been divided into classes of individuals, each of which at the time of writing (around 1830) received an allowance: those between 21 and 30 received £10 per annum; between 30 and 45, £20; between 45 and 55, £40; and upwards of 55, £60. There were extra allowances for younger classes who were ill or unable to work.

It was the means testing employed by the charity that irked Charles Gwilt: 'It is difficult to understand what is meant by behaviour. Who is to be the judge of proper behaviour in the kindred? The trustees have nothing to do with it. They cannot produce any deed in which such power is given them. The directions about this trust are all contained in the will, and there is certainly nothing about behaviour there.'

KEEPING TO THE RULES

The question of how recipients of Smith's Charity grants should be applied to the original letter of the will continued to be an important question in a period when charities and charitable giving became increasingly codified and regulated.

Monitoring the charity as to how its application accorded correctly to the terms of the will increased during this period. Charities such as Smith's were coming under increasing scrutiny from outside monitors: an inspector's report of 1825 took careful note of the administration costs of the charity (paid from the income from the manor at Longney and the Silver Street house – then let to a Mr Grouchy), which included the salaries of the clerk/treasurer and the surveyor and two dinners a year for the meeting of the trustees; the rest was a number of small expenses. The report noted disapprovingly that it was difficult to calculate the expenditure of each estate as the accounts were totted up as a general fund: 'the treasurer has undertaken to make out a correct amount of receipts and expenditure of each estate respectively, since he was first appointed to that office; and in future the balances will be entered in several books . . .'

Not all the parishes proved to the commissioners' satisfaction to be conforming to Henry's original wishes. Many of the parishes continued to distribute clothing or bread but a large number of them were found to be handing out small sums of cash. In Chiddingfold, for example, and in the parishes of Haslemere, Puttenham, Witley, Thursley and Send, the commissioners found that the parish overseers were 'ignorant' of the terms of Smith's will and as well as giving money were often giving it to people already receiving parochial relief. The parish of Egham, they noted approvingly, had already received a communication on the matter and had changed its ways and returned to bread and greatcoats.

In some of the parishes it was found that the overseers had developed new forms of distribution. These did not always correspond to the original designs of the will but they met with more approval than cash handouts. In Thorpe and in Chertsey, for instance, the commissioners found that 'it has been the course of this parish, to lay out the sum annually received on account of Smith's charity (which for the year 1822 was £57 6s and 2d) in the purchase of coals, and to sell these coals to the poor in winter at a low price. This course, which has been long pursued, appears to be a very beneficial mode of dispensing the charity; but it is certainly at variance with the particular directions given by Mr Smith.'

In Pirford, the parish gave out 'tickets' which acted as food stamps and entitled the bearer to bread,

Witham, near Braintree, where the breakaway trustees of Essex held their annual meetings. Engraving, *c.*1832.

In 1810, Henry Smith was among the benefactors of Wandsworth that were featured on a new balcony gallery in All Saints. It appears that although the £500 gift had disappeared, Wandsworth now received a grant from the Stoughton estate.

meat or flour. In East Horsley they sometimes distributed bread – but in other years when the need for food was less pressing, the churchwardens purchased faggots with their grant that they then distributed to the needy throughout the year, as required. In Windlesham, the parish overseers had stopped distributing bread since the village was enclosed and had started instead giving tools or 'implements of husbandry' to enable the poor to cultivate the remaining wasteland. The commissioners noted this initiative with approval but were forced also to add that it was not strictly in compliance with the letter of Henry Smith's will.

THE ESSEX FACTION

When it came to conforming to the stipulations laid out in Henry's will, the Essex trustees had from the mid eighteenth century demonstrated a keen interest in the parishes' compliance – and they were praised for it in the 1825 report. In 1743, for example, the trustees had noted in their accounts that Southover parish in Sussex had used their £10 to put two boys to apprenticeship and would thus be penalised by a year's suspension of their grant. In 1752, the trustees wrote to the parish overseers of Rotherfield reminding them that they were to distribute only upper garments and that they should have the initials HS embroidered on them. In Thetford in 1835, when badging of this kind had become infrequent, the overseers were still sewing the letter S on greatcoats purchased as part of the Smith bequest.

By 1801, the Essex trustees, after their annual audit meeting at the Blue Inn, Witham, had decided that a copy of Henry Smith's Deed should be sent to every parish under the Tolleshunt D'Arcy bequest – to remind the churchwardens and officiating clergyman of its regulations; it was to be pinned to the wall of the church. In 1815, the Revd Charles Gaunt, then curate of Fletching in Sussex, received a letter from the Essex trustees noting that the clothing distributed by the parish that year was 'inadmissible as respects the Items of Clothing which follow, viz. Trousers, Breeches, Shoes, hats, & hose'. Gaunt had clearly been reading up on the earlier Henry Smith deeds of uses, because in the same year the trustees wrote to tell him that they were not aware of any deed that permitted its application to putting out apprentices or giving portions to young women upon marriage. They also wrote to the vicar of Fletching hoping that none of the recipients of the charity were also on parish relief – a stipulation quite outside those laid down by Henry Smith.

The Sussex parishes, by this time thoroughly annoyed by the far-off Essex cabal and their interfering ways, served a suit alleging mismanagement in 1812, the complicated machinations of which continued until 1825. Their chief complaint was that the rent earned by Tolleshunt D'Arcy was set too low (£150 per year). By January 1816, the complainants were shown proof by the trustees that the estate had been assessed by a surveyor and that the tenant of Tolleshunt D'Arcy had agreed to take the farm for £430 per annum, and would insure the buildings at his own expense to the amount of £1,000. As it turned out, by Michaelmas 1817 the rent had dropped to £380 per annum, of which almost £100 went on lawyers' bills, leaving only £262 to be distributed among the parishes. Although there were attempts to raise the rent again, the tenant applied for another reduction, arguing 'owing to the pressure of the time he is wholly unequal to paying it without ruining himself'. In 1823, the rent had dropped to only £350 a year.

The solution to the long-running Tolleshunt dispute was perhaps the simplest of all. By 1825, the Essex parishes had gone their own way and the Sussex parishes had been absorbed into the main charity. And it has stayed that way ever since.

HARD TIMES

The period following 1815 and the end of the Napoleonic Wars was a time of national economic hardship – particularly hitting the agricultural poor. Returning soldiers and militiamen added to the number of men in search of work. By 1831, the population had grown from nine million at the end of the eighteenth century to fourteen million. Food was insufficient and expensive, so low wages meant lethargic workers who were not able to earn anything more than low wages. Industrialisation brought a prevalence of adulterated food: processed white bread flour was often mixed with alum. Labouring men lived on little but bread, cheese and perhaps some bacon or an onion (thought to be good for the blood) and women and children on sometimes nothing more than burnt toast soaked in hot water.

The rapid population growth and the widespread unemployment were met by escalating demands on the structures of poor relief. There was therefore outside pressure to make poor relief 'degrading', to insist on the application of utilitarian principles of distribution to make sure that the 'idle' were not rewarded. Relief would often be withheld from the able-bodied who would not enter a workhouse. This led to the introduction of workhouses on a far larger scale than had been known in the eighteenth century. The recommendations of a report on poor relief that was to form the basis of the Poor Law Amendment Act of 1834 suggested that the parish was no longer the most efficient means of managing poor relief. Parishes would continue to levy poor rates but the administration of new workhouses would be the responsibility of new unions into which the parishes were grouped. At Shere, for example, the existing poorhouse would be sold and those parishioners who applied for poor relief would be sent to a huge, newly built workhouse in Guildford, designed by George Gilbert Scott.

In this climate, when the shame of pauperism was now attendant on poor relief, private benefactions such as Henry Smith's represented a different face to the harsh and humiliating one of the workhouse. In 1856, the churchwardens of St Thomas the Apostle in Southwark received £16 cash, their grant for that year from the Kempsing estate. With it, they bought 252 pounds of meat, 100 loaves of bread, 29 yards of flannel, 20cwt of coal and six pairs of shoes. These they distributed among fifty-five families.[59] In Petersham, another Smith's Charity parish, they spent their grant on loaves of bread and coal. The account books show how many of the applicants were men with trades and skills – in 1866, recipients include two labourers, two 'infirm', a 'cripple' (but also a shoemaker), two gardeners, a woodman, a washerwoman, a carpenter and three bargemen. The previous year, the distribution had included six of those 'past work' who were inhabitants of the parish's existing almshouses.

THE INSPECTORS

In 1873, Charles Dickens, son of the novelist, lived for a while in Richmond upon Thames and became interested in the story of the local benefactor Henry 'Dog' Smith. Dickens wrote an account in the periodical *All the Year Round* of his 'investigations' into Smith. In his perambulations round the Surrey parishes, he found that most people happily subscribed to the Dog Smith legend: that in fact it had become emblematic of an imaginary gentler age of giving. In Epsom, where Smith's will was hung on the wall of St Martin's church, the novelist met an old man, 'a venerable beggar out on leave from a union workhouse', who told him with certainty that 'Smith was a beggar, there was no mistake about that . . . Ax anybody you like who knows anything, and they'll tell you that he was whipped for begging, and a great shame too.' In Mickleham, Dickens noted, the money of Henry Smith continued to be employed in 'relieving the distresses of the aged and infirm poor, and in other meritorious actions'.

Dickens' article reads like an unashamedly nostalgic lament for that loose, unregulated form of charitable giving in rural communities that had predated the New Poor Law Acts and the 1853 establishment of the Charity Commission. Private charities such as Smith's had become increasingly tangled in bureaucratic red tape and subject to outside monitoring; they were often the focus of accusations that their small doles created the idleness that the workhouse was designed to prevent. In 1868, the Charity Commissioners' report was stinging in its conclusions on many of the workings of Smith's Charity – and in it we see a new challenge of centralised accountability for independent charities. Apparent too is an ideological clash between two moral imperatives: on the one hand the administering of relief as it was called for and on the other the perceived threat to self-reliance that this raised – that charitable hand-outs actually fostered other social ills such as idleness and vagrancy. The commissioners sent inspectors to the Smith's Charity parishes to find out who was receiving the benefit of the charity's grant and in what form it was given.

In Fetcham, for example, which had a population of 390 and an annual grant of £52, the inspector noted that the parish distributed eighty loaves a week for ten weeks – but that the recipients were often also on the parish (a situation disapproved of by Charity Commission inspectors but quite in the tradition of parish benefactions), that 'improper persons ask for it' and that 'the charity is often taken as a right'. In Godalming, the inspector found that the parish distributed to about 500 people small amounts of cash and, to those who they thought unreliable with money, food tickets; the vicar had cut the number of recipients from 600 'and was in consequence abused, both in the vestry and in the street, by disappointed and discontented persons . . .' In Ewell, the vicar had instituted a mutual savings bank by which the parish added proportional cash amounts to deposits, thus encouraging saving. In Lichfield, the report said the parish overseers handed out petticoats and shoes, in contravention of the terms of the will, and that recipients now regarded these as an entitlement. 'The gifts . . . have turned half the inhabitants of Lichfield into beggars, hence idleness, drunkenness, poaching and thieving.'

The report singled out for approval Hartlepool, which like Reigate had redirected its Smith's Charity funds towards education by a scheme established by the Court of Chancery. The trustees gave Hartlepool £200 a year, half of which went to support the grammar school there (still called the Henry Smith School) and the other half to a hospital.

The report had concluded that educational subsidies (an aspect of relief not covered by the terms of Henry's will) were preferable to food, clothing or cash handouts. In Stafford the inspector found that, against the rules set by the trustees, they had been spending their grant on paying skilled workers to take on young boys as apprentices. Here, as in many of the parishes, they found among those they questioned a general sense that the old form of distribution, of 'dole', was no longer working satisfactorily. Yet the solution was punitive: the threat of the workhouse.

A Soldier's Return by George Morland (1763–1804).Vagrant and penniless former soldiers were often forced to beg for parish relief.

The authors of the 1868 report also criticised the way in which the fund for poor clergy was administered. The number of recipient clergymen had grown over the centuries and so had their grants. In 1698, poor clergy near Alfriston received about £5 a year; in 1800, they received £12 a year at Christmas; in 1811, fifteen clergyman received £15 each; and by 1819, recipients received £20 each. (In the six years leading up to 1816, the commissioners reported that Alfriston produced £2,800 in allowances to poor clergy.) The commissioners concluded that it would be more effective if taken away from the hard-pressed treasurer of Smith's Charity and reorganised as part of a government office:

> the observations we have to make are these. In the first place, the amount of trouble and expense, not only to the charity, but also to a great number of candidates for it, arising from the issuing of circulars, the sending in of applications, the procuring of certificates, the sifting of cases, and other negotiations, is very considerable. Secondly, the excitement of hope and the disappointment of failure, is apt to have a painful and deteriorating effect; it introduces an element of chance into necessity of making such applications, familiarises the mind with the practice of begging, and too often with that putting a false colour on a case by the suppression of facts which, if known, would tell against the application. We cannot help thinking it would be a better mode of spending the funds, and would produce no conceivable injustice to either dead or living – indeed it would seem more in accordance with the founder's views – if the tithes were sold, and the proceeds handed over to either the Ecclesiastical Commissioners or the governors of Queen Anne's Bounty for the augmentation of incumbencies in poor and populaces places. This would benefit the very classes for whom the benefit is designed, and for whom it is now confined, while the recipients of it would take the benefit without feeling they were owing anything to voluntary gifts, or with any loss of self respect, on the contrary with the satisfaction of knowing that they

were paid, and honourably earning, at least as much as they were receiving.

The 1868 report demonstrates how extensively the climate of charitable giving had changed in the wake of the new poor laws. The emphasis was now on giving in order to inculcate moral growth: 'We have indicated how the funds might be turned to good purposes, such as schools and hospitals and clubs for clothing or savings. They might be made to confer the healthy mind and the healthy body and those habits of thrift and forethought without which poverty and squalid distress might come. This might be done not only without injustice to any living person, but even with more regard to the founder's special directions, certainly with far more regard to the spirit of his gifts.'

The administration of grants to the poor kindred came in for particular criticism. The numbers of registered descendants of Joan Jackson had gone from four names in 1700 to 412 in 1868. The commissioners attached to their report a list that showed the number of 'greats' that could be added to the modern kindred to denote their relationship to Henry: by the 1860s, the registered kindred ranged from six to ten greats covering a vast range of incomes and circumstances. The authors of the report evidently believed that this made the bequest difficult to administer justly – or without more rigorous intervention. Money advanced to help with work or training, they wrote, often led to 'improvident speculations', which had led recipients further into debt; how could the trustees truly judge who was idle on their allowance and who was industrious?; 'What is to be the test of such poverty as comes within the words of the will?' they asked.

The report went on to list some of the questionable applications made by the kindred: 'S.O.W is described as ragged and destitute. He is paid weekly. According to his own account he has been dying of consumption for above 20 years;' 'H.M is an actor, a refreshment-house keeper, and a cupper. He returns no income. He applied for assistance to go to a watering-place;' 'F.T.A applied for the payment of a governess for his children.' A brass and ivory turner applied to Smith's for money that would pay for his daughter to learn music. Examples of poor behaviour, such as debt (applicants arriving for their cash grant with their creditors), drunkenness, errant husbands failing to support their families and a demanding letter from a member of the kindred living comfortably in St James's, were produced as exemplars of 'the way in which the spirit of independence is sapped'.

The report concluded that the only fair way of apportioning the poor kindred's money was either to distribute it equally between all the registered kindred – without resorting to tests of 'need' – or to dispense with the fund altogether (and it is clear that this is the report's authors' preferred solution) as, they maintained, 'there is nothing to show that he [Henry Smith] looked beyond his own generation.'

REGULATION

In 1875, the Charity Commission presented the trustees of Smith's Charity with a draft Scheme, drawn up by the commissioners, that would properly regulate the wealth of the charity and its efficient distribution. The trustees, led by Henry, Duke of Northumberland, argued that their current operations could not be changed except by sanction of Chancery; the case was heard between 1875 and 1878, and introduced by the Attorney General with this summary: 'This action had become necessary on account of the rapidly increasing income of the Charity, and the large number of persons, about 700, claiming to be the testator's "kindred", only some of whom were possessed of the qualifications prescribed by the will, of being sick, aged, and impotent persons and such as were not able to work for a living.'

The burning question, sparked by the 1868 report, parts of which were read out in court, was whether a portion of the income of the Kensington estate should be used, as the commissioners were demanding, for charitable purposes other than the kindred – and if so, how much of it and for whom. The lawyers acting for the Attorney General were of the opinion that any surplus funds should be directed to the relief directly of poverty, 'poverty being the main object the testator had in view'.

The trustees, however, argued that they should be permitted to use the money for a wider remit: the education of poor children, giving priority to the children of the poorest kindred, a line they were already pursuing – that very year they had paid for the education of sixty-six kindred children. There was some doubt in court, however, that the trustees' definition of 'poor' could be classified as comprising destitution. Mr Jessel, for the Attorney General, wondered: 'A gift which is not a gift to the poor, is not a charity. How for instance could a gift to the "poorest of the Dukes of Northumberland" be a charity?' In 1877, the conclusion of the court was that the surplus income should be directed into other charitable causes: 'such income is applicable for the benefit of charitable objects other than kindred of the testator.'

A regulatory Scheme was finalised in 1889. In it, the trustees of Henry's charity committed to its following detailed procedures when it came to holding regular meetings, appointment of trustees and voting for new measures. It laid out the duties of the surveyor, the treasurer and those of the clerk, who was bound to take minutes of every meeting. Fireproof boxes were to hold the account books and deeds of the charity, which were henceforth to be audited and preserved. Finally the Scheme introduced regulations on trustees not holding or leasing charity property (a rule that would have caused consternation among Henry's original trustees).

Relief of the Unemployed in London. A picture from the *Illustrated London News* of 13 March 1886 shows the poor being given soup tickets.

The rules governing grants to the kindred were also codified. No one between the ages of 45 and 55, for example, would be allowed to receive an annual allowance in excess of £40 and no one above the age of 55 in excess of £60. Widows of kindred were to be recognised as kin as long as they remained widows. There was some encouragement to use existing institutions for kindred in need, paying for their upkeep if necessary: thus a suitable list was compiled, including asylums, orphanages, hospitals for the incurable and convalescent homes. The total amount spent by the charity on the education of younger kindred was not to exceed £3,000.

The new Scheme also allowed that £5,000 could every year, at the trustees' discretion, be transferred to the fund for the relief and maintenance of godly preachers – which would then be called the Clergy Trust. The rest of the income, after the kindred's share had been apportioned, was now released for other causes that were judged to be properly concerned with the relief of dire poverty.

FASHIONABLE KENSINGTON

As the case in Chancery had emphasised, the Kensington estate had grown during the middle of the century beyond all recognition. During the 1820s, Brompton and its surroundings were still very much an outer edge of London, still pastoral, with grazing lands and fields as well as villas and gardens. Nursery planting was still the predominant form of cultivation: John Middleton, the agriculturalist, in 1798 commented that 'At Chelsea, Brompton, Kensington, Hackney, Dalston, Bow and Mile End, much ground is occupied by nurserymen, who spare no expense in collecting the choicest sort, and greatest variety of fruit-trees, and ornamental shrubs and flowers, from every quarter of the globe; and which they cultivate in a high degree of perfection ... Many of them are annually exported to Ireland, Spain, Portugal, Italy, Russia, and, until lately, to France.'[60] An early nineteenth-century author, describing a voyage from Brompton to Brentford, noted how as he went west towards Brompton there were signs that 'you are exchanging the smoke and filth of

The Queen's Elm, Fulham Road, in the mid nineteenth century, showing a sign for a nursery garden.

Earls Court Farm, just over the border of Smith's Kensington estate. It consisted of 190 acres and was demolished in 1878 to make way for Earls Court Underground station. Watercolour, mid nineteenth century.

the metropolis for the salubrious breezes and refreshing verdure of rural scenery'. The parish boundary between Kensington and Chelsea was until the 1840s marked by a hedgerow.

In 1820, despite Novosielski's developments, the village of Brompton still maintained large acres under cultivation, mainly for nursery gardens: Thomas Faulkner in his *History of Kensington* (1820) recorded six acres of nursery gardens on the Smith estate that belonged to Mr Gibbs. They were

> laid out for horticultural and agricultural experimental purposes: the latter are divided into upwards of eight hundred compartments, each two feet square, bordered with box and separated by a footpath, containing specimens of every vegetable at present known and used in farming including all the various kinds of corn, wheat, barley, oats, beans and green food for cattle. The collection of grasses is very extensive . . . There are extensive warehouses on the premises for the preservation of seeds.

In 1829, however, the rural seclusion of Brompton began its final transformation with the appointment of George Basevi as architect for the Smith's Charity Kensington estate.

Basevi was, at the time of his appointment to Smith's, 35 years old and had been working as architect and surveyor for the adjoining Thurloe estate since 1827 (he orchestrated the creation of Thurloe Square in 1839). He had already built up a successful architectural practice: one of Basevi's first commissions was Gatcombe Park in Gloucestershire. The trustees therefore invited him to succeed William

'Elevation for the six shops in Fulham Road' by George Basevi, *c.*1836.

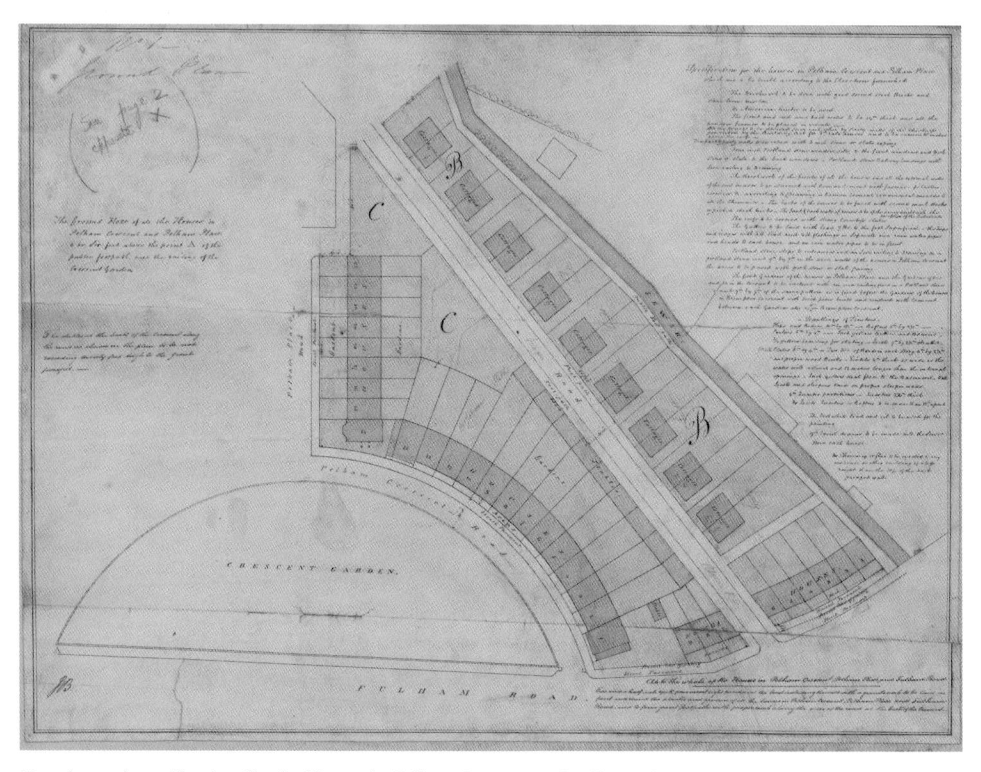

Site plan and specification 'for the Houses in Pelham Crescent and Pelham Place' by George Basevi, *c.*1836.

Clutton, son of the surveyor, who had recently retired, with a view to further developing the land in Kensington.

A former pupil of Sir John Soane and a first cousin of Benjamin Disraeli, Basevi was described by a contemporary as 'cold and somewhat haughty'. On his appointment, his first job for the trustees was the unglamorous planning of an improved sewage system to be laid under Novosielski's houses in Michael's Grove and Brompton Crescent. This went ahead in 1829 at a cost of £450. Basevi then produced a comprehensive plan for the redevelopment of the estate, which he presented to the trustees at the end of 1829. His plan incorporated two of the remaining nurseries – Harrison and Bristow's nursery and Gibbs's – and was bounded by Love Lane, on the Chelsea borders in the north-east, and by the Fulham Road in the south. The plots were leased in 1833 (with some complications, as the current inhabitants had to be negotiated out of the years remaining on their leases) to the builder James Bonnin – another individual who left a decisive stamp on the transformation of the Kensington estate.

At the time he secured the leases, Bonnin was in his fifties. Of Huguenot extraction and described as a builder, undertaker and carpenter – and latterly a successful timber merchant – Bonnin had been involved in development work with Smith's Charity since 1822, building for them a row of eight houses called Onslow Terrace (later demolished to make way for the underground railway). On leasing the Smith's sites he was committed to building houses there to Basevi's precise specifications – laying out a

Onslow Square in 1851. Charles Freake insisted that the houses had straight chimneys because he believed that soot in crooked ones caused cancer of the scrotum in child chimney sweeps.

The Bell and Horns inn in 1853 still looked leafy and secluded.

By 1914, the Bell and Horns had become a substantial public house next to South Kensington tube station, which had opened in 1868.

square or garden 'to be called Pelham Crescent . . . Inclosed by an iron railing'. The crescent would run over what were still the gardens of Brompton Grange. Between 1833 and 1844, Bonnin, with his son, James Bonnin junior, oversaw the creation, to Basevi's designs, of dozens of stucco-faced houses with pitched roofs, for Pelham Crescent, Pelham Place and most of Pelham Street.

Development of the area went at a furious pace – with speculating lessees among others keen to make a profit from it. Bonnin was among those whose finances were stung by reckless over-expansion. In 1846 he declared himself bankrupt and had to apply to the Kensington Board of Guardians for £10 to pay for him to travel to Australia to live with his daughter; he died days after his arrival.

Observing the sudden emergence in 1833–4 of a small row of cottages called Sussex Terrace, George Godwin wrote in the periodical *The Builder* that it was 'considered a somewhat, if not doubtful, speculation so little dreamt of was that change in the value of land which ultimately turned the locality into a vast and populous resort'.

By 1843, St Saviour's church had been built on part of what had once been Quail's field, and to its north-east, two facing terraces called Walton Place, named after George Walton Onslow, one of the Smith's trustees. Work was halted briefly in 1845, when George Basevi died suddenly at the age of 49, after falling through a hole in the floor of the bell tower of Ely Cathedral while inspecting repairs there. Reginald Bray, the Smith's treasurer, that same year invited Henry Clutton, an architect and the grandson of old William Clutton of Hartswood, to become the surveyor of the Kensington estate. With his brother John Clutton, who became perhaps the most famous surveyor of Victorian London, Henry was a central figure in the earliest years of the creation of modern Kensington. It was he who gave his approval for the development plans of the person who more than anyone else was to transform Smith's estate of muddy market gardens into the fashionable urban residential centre it is now.

SIR CHARLES FREAKE

Charles James Freake was a highly coloured London figure, with a ruthless flair for speculation and a talent for seizing the opportunities offered by the city's rapid expansion. The son of a London wine merchant, by the time he was 25 Freake had borrowed large sums of money and with them, in a single year in 1844, had built several houses in Chester Terrace, Belgravia. On these he was then able to raise £14,000 for his next development project.

Freake had had an eye on the Smith's estate for some time before he approached Henry Clutton for

Sir Charles Freake at the height of his celebrated career. Cartoon lithograph by Theobald Chartran (1849–1907).

JOHN CLUTTON

John Clutton, surveyor for the Kensington estate. Clutton was a much-loved and respected figure, whose butler recalled his saying: 'James, I am lunching with Mr Robert today, remind me to take my teeth.'

The future and management of the South Kensington estate rested during the nineteenth century with another of William Clutton's sons, John, born in 1809. John Clutton became a legend in his profession, one of the most successful surveyors in London, a 'most unheard-of success', as he himself described it in his memoir.

John Clutton claimed to have had only a piecemeal education at Cuckfield grammar school and even at the height of his career he wrote: 'I have a hundred times felt my inferiority when mixing with educated men.' At 17, he went to work with his father (as apprentice) in exchange for £50 per annum. 'My time', he recalled, 'was spent principally in farming and learning land agency – viz. timber valuations, receipts of rents, etc.'

On the death of his father, Clutton was 30 years old and recently married – 'my marriage has been one of unvaried good' – despite the tangle of debts left by his father's business. William bequeathed John £3,000, with which he set up an office in London, taking its name from the firm in Reigate and calling it William Clutton & Sons, at 8 Parliament Street. Here they also lived, employing one clerk, and they were soon joined by Robert Spencer, who was to be his close ally and partner. The main task of his business then was purchasing land for the South Eastern Railway Company.

By 1844, the business was earning enough for the family to move to a house in Whitehall Place and then another one in Sussex Square. By 1851, the business was called simply Messrs Clutton and was an entirely separate concern from the one in Reigate.

John Clutton was, by all contemporary accounts of him, held in great affection. Asked why he always paid his clerks more than their stipulated wage, he claimed never, ever to have sacked anyone. 'I have always considered what I should feel myself, knowing, as I do also, how little they have to fall back on.' A typical Clutton piece of wisdom was: 'Honey catches more flies than vinegar.' He bred pedigree cattle at his country house in Hertfordshire, habitually wore an ulster cape and liked his coachman to tear along country roads at top speed. He was a plain speaker, 'the sworn enemy of adjectives', according to an office memoir, and a modest demeanour hid a keen business brain. Once asked for the cause of his great success, he said it was a daily half-hour of reading, particularly Cobbett's English Grammar. 'Are you infallible Mr Clutton? Do you never make mistakes?' 'Oh yes,' he replied, 'but then I do more business than most men.'

approval to build Onslow Square, Onslow Crescent and the (now demolished) Onslow Houses. George Basevi had already produced plans for Onslow Square – to which Freake added only some embellishments.

The first rates on the houses in Onslow Square were paid in 1846, and by 1850 almost all of them were tenanted. By the mid 1850s, Freake extended Onslow Square even further west by building over land that had once been a nursery garden. Hale House, once the home of Sir William Blake, was demolished in 1850. The 12.5-acre site on which it had stood, which also contained Brompton Park House, was also demolished and its land absorbed into the site of the Victoria and Albert Museum, part of which opened in 1857. The trustees also relinquished a pocket of land on the north side of the Brompton Road, known as 'the carpet ground' for its scrubbiness, for use by the Commissioners of the Great Exhibition. In exchange they received a similar sized pocket on the south side – which became the western end of Cranley Place, Onslow Gardens and, in the end, Cranley Gardens. The 1874 account books show receipts for the Kensington estate that are dominated by leases taken by Freake: he paid nearly £4,000 a year to Smith's for them.

Not everyone was delighted by the newness of Freake's Brompton. A poet called E. Yates lamented the sprouting of 'Gaunt, stuccoed houses, glowing white/ And many a turfed and railinged square;' and in 1853, Cardinal Newman complained that the site selected for the future Brompton Oratory was in 'a neighbourhood of second-rate gentry and second-rate shops'. William Makepeace Thackeray, the novelist, was more enthusiastic about the area, at least at first: in 1852, at the height of his popularity, he bought the lease on number 36 Onslow Square for £2,100 and declared it a 'pretty little house looking into a very pretty little square'. By 1858 Thackeray had decided that the house was 'shabby genteel' and he moved to a large house he had built in Kensington Palace Green – dying there four years later.

St Paul's, Onslow Square. In 1859, the trustees of Smith's Charity donated a plot of land on which to build a church, Freake funding part of the costs himself. Consecrated in 1860, St Paul's could hold a congregation of 1,550 – and most seats were rented out for an annual sum.

Opposite the Thackerays lived their great friends Sir Theodore Martin and his wife, who took up residence in number 51 and stayed there for fifty-eight years. As an indication of just how spacious the Martins' house was, Helena Martin described one of their many dinner parties as 'About 56 present and not crowded', while Arthur Munby, the Victorian lawyer best known now for his close interest in the sexual health of domestic servants, wrote in his diary that the house was 'one of the most charming in London. It has a lofty spacious hall made more beautiful by pictures and statues; and a noble staircase, sloping

A 1903 photograph of the building of the front entrance of the Victoria and Albert Museum on Cromwell Road; the Natural History Museum is in the background.

up round three sides of it, leads to a suite of drawing-rooms furnished with costly and most fastidious elegance'.

Freake himself also – in 1860 – departed his house in Onslow Square and took up residence in a large, double-fronted mansion next to what was to become the Natural History Museum. It was called Cromwell House and here Freake (who received a baronetcy in 1873) entertained lavishly. He and his wife were particularly fond of the fashionable Victorian entertainment of *tableaux vivants*, in which visitors and guests posed, in stage-like settings, in stirring scenes from literature and history. The Freakes installed a claret-coloured velvet 'frame' in their drawing room for these occasions. During one evening at Cromwell House in 1880, Lily Langtry herself appeared in a *tableau vivant* depicting scenes from the novels of Sir Walter Scott – watched by an audience which included the Prince and Princess of Wales.

Sir Charles Freake died in 1884, leaving an estate worth £700,000. He was buried in Brompton cemetery and a tablet to his memory is in St Paul's, Onslow Square.

8

The Twentieth Century

By the turn of the twentieth century, the effects of the Scheme instituted in 1889 were fully evident. A few representatives of the kindred had not relinquished the kindred's share of the larger portion of the Kensington estate without opposition. There survives a curious collection of articles from 1908 published in a long defunct journal called *You and I*, in which the kindred's cause is taken up by an anonymous champion. Entitled 'Millions for the Smiths', the author made wild claims that the trustees had in the early years of the charity sold off vastly valuable estates that by right belonged to the kindred. The articles encouraged the kindred to put up a case for their rightful claims on the estate – but nothing has been unearthed to tell us whether anyone actually did.

Most of the income from the Kensington estate was now applied to grants for larger charitable purposes. In 1911, the estate gave away £9,000 to charitable causes after payments to the kindred (including for them subsidies for technical education, an area that had been encouraged in the 1889 Scheme) and the trustees dealt directly with distributions to hospitals that were the beneficiaries.

There was also the issue of surplus in the other estates' annual income. In 1903, a new Scheme provided that any surplus income left over 'after payment of the authorised sums is applied in making

The Children's Country Holiday Fund was one of the first charities to receive a grant from Smith's Charity after the Scheme of 1889 expanded its remit. Here, a group of children set off on holiday in 1900.

grants to hospitals within the counties or areas in which any part of the property is situate, and convalescent homes'. In 1907, the treasurer wrote to the trustees saying 'we would again draw your attention to the large balance you have in hand.'

The range of charitable causes had expanded, a reflection of a period in which private charity operated on a far larger scale. Smith's still had to adhere closely to the definition of the terms of Henry's will but there continued to be discussion about how these could be best interpreted for a new age.

In 1907, for example, Warrens the solicitors (descendants of William Bray's old firm) wrote to the trustees to express concern that the Surrey parish of Stoke D'Abernon was using its annual gift of £4 10s to encourage penny banks and that 'accumulation is outside the scope of the trust'. The trustees' response was that penny banks encouraged thrift and that Mr Blackburn, the vicar of Stoke D'Abernon, should be supported in his endeavours.

Country holidays for urban children were another theme that developed during this period. Smith's regularly gave sums to the Children's Country Holiday Fund (first known as the Children's Fresh Air Mission), started in 1877 by Samuel and Henrietta Barnett, the founders of Toynbee Hall. For slum children living in densely populated urban tenements in extreme poverty, who had never seen the sea or even a field, this was a remarkable operation. In 1914, the chairman of the CCHF published a letter in the Catholic journal *The Tablet*, telling its readers that there were 750,000 children who currently enjoyed a holiday in the fresh air thanks to the charity – and how desperately it needed funds as the numbers of children who needed it were growing every year.

Rural life in Surrey had changed its nature too in this period – and though rapid development had changed the appearance and demography of much of the county, there was still a pressing poverty in many parishes.

George Sturt, a wheelwright in Farnham, has left one of the most vivid observational accounts of Surrey village life before the First World War. Writing as George Bourne, Sturt examined the shift in parish life from a communal economy to a market economy, watching how the arrival of golf courses and commuter belt villas had brought a surface prosperity but also a loss of confidence and self-reliance in many rural workers.

It is a decline that Sturt attributes at least in part to the enclosure of the commons. Employment was now subject to forces far beyond the control of the parish. In Farnham, forty men had been employed on the railway but when the line was completed they were thrown overnight out of work. Sturt found particularly that traditional working opportunities for women had declined, leaving them no option but to take up the ill-paid drudgery of life in domestic service in one of the new villas that had sprung up around Farnham. Taking in washing, which had been a means of earning pennies, had been displaced by the new steam laundries that were popular in the suburbs.

> Field work still employs a few women, although every year their numbers decrease. It is miserably paid at a shilling a day, or in some cases on piecework terms which hardly work out at a higher figure. Piecework, for instance, was customary in the hop gardens (now rapidly disappearing), where the women cut the bines and 'tied' or 'trained" the hops at so much per acre, providing their own rushes for the tying. At hay-making and at harvesting there is work for women; and again in the hop gardens, when the picking is over, women are useful at clearing up the bines. They can earn money too, at trimming swedes, picking up newly-dug potatoes, and so on; but when all is said, there are not many of them who can find work to do in the fields all the year round. At the best, bad weather often interrupts them, and the stress and hardships of the work, not to mention other drawbacks, make the small earnings from it a doubtful blessing.

THE FIRST WORLD WAR

The advent of the 1914 war inevitably brought several causes to the forefront of the trustees' notices. There were increased applications to Smith's for

A postcard of lavender being cut and bundled in Carshalton, Surrey, *c.*1905.

grants to hospitals and convalescent homes and for the supply of surgical appliances (as included in the 1889 Scheme). There were also individual situations that spoke of the upheaval and trauma of the war years. One registered member of the kindred, aged 63, wrote to say that although he earned £1 a week, he had to support an invalid wife, a 'feeble-minded' daughter and a son suffering from 'nervous disability' and was therefore left with almost nothing as spending money. His three sons were all in the army and the War Office made the family no payments. Another member of the kindred was given the money in 1914 to go to South Africa, where the sun was thought to be beneficial for his health. The trustees agreed to an allowance but war was declared and the trip was never made; in 1916, the trustees learned that he had died of TB.

In 1918, the surveyor Bernard Marr-Johnson (who had taken up the post in 1912 after the death of his uncle, Ralph Clutton) wrote to the trustees explaining the difficulties of collecting many of the South Kensington rents. The area was, he said, full of small antique dealers, whose shops and businesses had been seriously hit by the war – many of them were in arrears as a result. He enclosed a list of those to whom he thought 'leniency' should be extended.

THE 1920S

Tithes, such as those in Alfriston and Mayfield that provided the money for the poor clergy fund, were no longer as significant a source of income as they had once been. The fund was now annually topped up by money from the surplus of the Kensington estate. In 1912, the trustees' minutes record that the procedure for the poor clergy grants was still for applicant clergy to apply direct to the treasurer (enclosing a recommendation from their bishop). In 1927, however, the trustees decided that from that year they would invite the bishops whose dioceses took in those counties where Smith's Charity owned land to submit nominations for clergy grants.

South Kensington, despite having a reputation for being a rackety, even bohemian, neighbourhood, was still booming. Families were moving in, attracted to nearby parks (and Kensington Gardens in particular) and in 1920, the trustees approved an application for a perambulator shed in Sumner Place. In a reflection of the increase in private car ownership, these years

LIVE IN SURREY
AND BE HAPPY!
FREQUENT ELECTRIC TRAINS DAY AND NIGHT.
"THE COUNTRY AT LONDON'S DOOR,"
FREE AT ANY S.R. ENQUIRY OFFICE.
SOUTHERN
ELECTRIC

A 1926 poster advertising Southern Electric Railways. Surrey, once one of the poorest of the English counties, was by the mid twentieth century part of the prosperous London commuter belt. Poster by Ethelbert White (1891–1972).

also see a flurry of applications to build garages. The South Kensington Underground station had opened in 1868, where the Brompton turnpike (and its three coaching inns) had once stood. Over the years it had expanded: in 1885, the Metropolitan District Railway had opened an underground passageway to take visitors from the station to the new museums on the other side of the Cromwell Road – the Natural History and the Victoria and Albert. In 1929, however, several lessees wrote to the Smith's trustees asking if they could do something not about constant building work – but about the terrible noise issuing from the Undergound Electric Railways Dining Club in Pelham Place.

The income from the Kensington estate continued to provide the charity's main source of revenue. The Scheme of 1929 made small alterations to the criteria of awards for the kindred that had been laid out in the Scheme of 1889: including higher education on the list, for example. It also expanded the list of wider charitable grants that might be paid for by the estate – these included building projects for existing hospitals or charitable institutions (particularly for incurables). It stipulated too that special wings might be erected to house persons in need who had been nominated by the trustees. In a long list of possible recipients, the trustees reiterated their commitment to 'obtaining for the children of the poor in the administrative county of London the benefit of a visit for the country' and added war widows, and disabled ex-servicemen.

THE 1930S AND THE SECOND WORLD WAR

Smith's Charity saw two more significant appointments in the 1930s: Guy Gotto became treasurer and clerk of the charity in 1931 and Kenneth Marr-Johnson took over from his father as surveyor in 1937. These two were to steer the charity through the war and the post-war period right into the 1970s. Kenneth Marr-Johnson, looking back in 1968, recollected that when he first took up the job of surveyor, the Kensington estate was still let almost entirely on full repairing leases of the kind issued by William Bray – for an average of fourteen years each, 'except for two blocks of working class cottages in Crescent Place and Yeoman's Row and some mews flats'. It was not an exclusive neighbourhood in London, in fact quite mixed, but that Freake's South Kensington was affluent shows in the infant mortality rates registered in the Brompton ward, which were among the lowest in London: 3.2 per cent between 1932 and 1934.

In the mid 1930s, the charity twice refused the Anti-Slavery Society a grant on the grounds that Smith's did not give money to international causes.

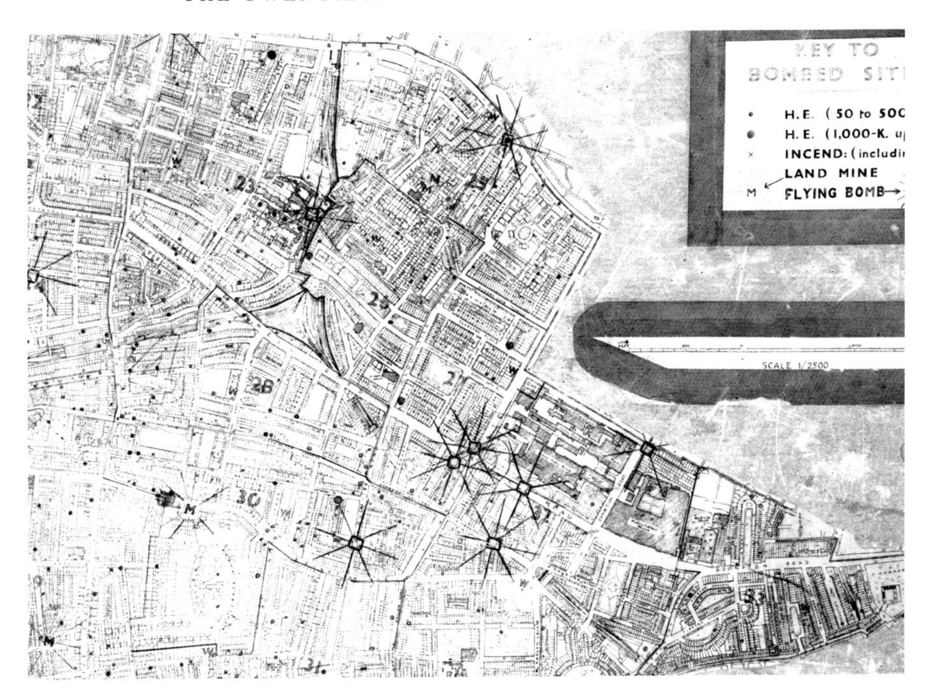

A map of Kensington in the Second World War. The crosses mark the places hit by German bombs.

The *Manchester Guardian* took up the case some years later, in 1953, and in an editorial questioned 'One would have thought that no contemporary cause could have been closer to the intention of the founder than that which the society exists to further.' Yet in 1952, an amended Scheme specifically included the following paragraph in the list of those who could apply for donations: 'Organisations, bodies or persons engaged in the restoration of slaves or serfs to their freedom or the relief or rehabilitation of freed slaves or serfs or their children or grandchildren or assisting freed slaves or serfs or their children or grandchildren to establish themselves in free society or preventing the seizure of human beings for slavery or serfdom or preventing the traffic in slaves or serfs or engaged in any of such purposes as aforesaid.' By the mid 1990s, donations to Anti-Slavery International were listed among the Henry Smith Charity's grants.

Substantial war damage had an effect on Kensington and Marr-Johnson described how difficult it had been to let large houses in Onslow Square in the period of the build-up to war.

> The war made havoc of the estate. Many of the lessees left their houses empty and disclaimed the leases as soon as there was any war damage. Those who stayed took in a number of paying guests. The leases in Onslow Square expired during the war and all the houses were requisitioned by the Ministry of Works together with the two gardens which they covered with huts, air-raid shelters and other temporary works. These were used at various times for Polish forces, Gibraltarian refugees and finally Irish workmen for coping with war damage. On other parts of the estate any habitable property that became empty was requisitioned by Kensington or Chelsea Council for emergency housing.[61]

The trustees initially resisted the local authorities attempts in 1941 to take away the iron railings on the estate for military recycling but eventually had no choice when they were requisitioned. The property standing on the site of Henry's house at Silver Street was reduced to rubble in the Blitz (and the site compulsorily purchased by the City of London corporation after the war).

But the greater effects came from the need for money for surgical appliances, for medical aid, for

A depiction of Silver Street in ruins after an attack during the Blitz. Watercolour by war artist Dennis Flanders (1915–94).

convalescent charities and for individual victims of the effects of war. Between 1939 and 1940, twenty-four hospitals received grants ranging from £75 to £10,000. Some boys from the village of Arborfield in Berkshire wrote, somewhat optimistically, to request that Smith's Charity would give them a sum of money to buy books or games – they were being trained as mechanics in the Royal Army Ordnance Corps. In 1939, an elderly clergyman wrote to the trustees that his pension had been reduced and that he was the sole support of an invalid wife and daughter: 'I would be glad of a gift from your society.' Another wrote to say he was almost destitute and that it was the worst year since he was ordained in 1904.

During and after the war, the parishes had to cope with the burden of rationing. In Putney, in the parish of St Mary's, during the 1940s and 50s they continued to use their Smith's grant to distribute coats for men (another Putney charity provided dresses for women). They paid for the coats to be made up by a local tailor, Stanley Silcock. In 1941, thirteen coats were given away to men ranging in age from 63 to 84 years. Local visitors left careful notes in the account books. They were then submitted to the scrutiny of the churchwardens and other trustees. Fifty years later it is not always clear what criteria is being applied in the selection – but the efficacy of local knowledge was the reason that Henry Smith established the system of local trustees in the first place.

> [Mr X], aged 69 and a half, living off old age pension of 26s a week and national assistance of 16s. rent 14s 3d. lived in Putney 40 yrs, bad bronchial asthma, has no coat only mackintosh, worked for London transport for 25 years and wd have got a pension if he'd stayed another five years. Visitor notes that he was lonely and needed cheering up. Had never had a coat before. He got a 'YES' pencilled strongly across his report.
>
> [Mr Y], however, of the Lower Richmond Road, aged 67, had never had a coat, had lived in Putney all his life and his family for three generations. His wife was bedridden with ulcerate legs and he did all the care work, cooking and shopping. His rent was £4.18.5 weekly, rates £5.18.5 quarterly. Income – old age pension £12 and his weekly national assistance £1.19.6 weekly. A pencilled note, heavily underlined three times reads 'Emphatically No! NO! NO!'[62]

Successful applicants had to supply their own clothing coupons, which were then used for the purchasing of the coats. Clothes rationing came to an end in 1949, but in 1950 the Putney trustees were dismayed to find that the amount of their annual grant from Smith's (which came from the Kempsing estate) had been reduced. As they had already ordered their coats for that year, they were concerned they would not be able to pay the bill. They wrote to Guy Gotto and he replied explaining that due to a change in investments the amount divisible between the parishes had decreased: owing to the sale of war stock and the reinvestment in savings' bonds the income for the parishes had that year been cut.[63] In 1948, the trustees published a Scheme by which kindred in possession of an income of more than £400 a year would not be permitted to claim from the charity.

During the 1950s, small events logged by the trustees' minutes nonetheless show the huge social changes of the post-war years. In 1948, Smith's allowed doctors employed in the new National Health Service to use premises owned by the charity in Kensington. According to the trustees' minutes of that year:

> It has been the custom of the Trustees to grant licences to Medical Practitioners, who are lessees of their houses, to permit them to carry on their Practices on the premises, but to provide in such licences that they shall be revocable in the event of the doctor treating panel patients on the premises . . . On condition that nothing authorised by the licences shall cause any nuisance or annoyance to the Trustees, their Lessees, or tenants, or the neighbourhood.

In 1952, as part of the nationwide effort to try and solve the post-war housing crisis, the trustees agreed to build a block of social-housing flats in Yeoman's Row 'as a philanthropic object', on which they expected to reap only a two per cent return. It was the charity's only excursion into building projects in conjunction with Kensington Council.

FROM THE 1970S TO THE MILLENNIUM AND BEYOND

In the late 1960s, Kenneth Marr-Johnson had observed that rising costs and rents were making it difficult for the older tenants of the Kensington estate to meet the demands of higher rents. There were still, he said, some patches of old South Kensington remaining. 'Crescent Place is a delightful backwater of little houses which were originally the gardeners' cottages when the estate was a market garden. They have now all been modernised.'* It took decades for war damage to buildings to be fully repaired: in 1971, the Kensington trustees approved the replacement of railings in Pelham Place that had been removed during the war and the year after that they agreed to replace them in the communal squares and gardens on the estate. The matter of railings was still, however, being discussed in 1988.

Many of the old rules that had governed the workings of the charity at its seventeenth-century inception began to look archaic by the 1970s. The Archbishop of Canterbury, Donald Coggan, when he took office in 1974, was persuaded by many of the younger staff in Lambeth to purge from his schedule any nominal duties of patronage that seemed no longer to have a purpose. Dr Coggan received a letter from Jocelyn Hambro, then chairman of the trustees, who pointed out the importance of the Henry Smith Charity's historic connection with the archbishops of Canterbury. The archbishop changed his mind and the link between Lambeth Palace and the charity has been enthusiastically retained to this day – surviving the 1999 surrender by the Lord Chancellor's office of its role in the appointment of trustees.

In 1996, in perhaps the most dramatic move in its 400-year history, the trustees of the Henry Smith Charity (as Smith's Charity was now known) sold the Kensington estate to the medical charity the Wellcome Trust for £280 million. The purpose was partly to diversify the charity's investments and partly because of the increasing management required by changes in leasehold legislation during the 1990s.

This changed the shape of the charity's organisation considerably. The parishes' grants, for example, now come from the main fund – a situation that has corrected imbalances in the amounts received when

* A house in Crescent Place sold in May 2013 for £4.2 million.

they were dependent on the incomes from different estates. By 2008, the main grants Scheme of the Henry Smith Charity, disposed of at the discretion of the trustees, was £21 million, approximately double the amount that had been available before 1996.

INTO THE TWENTY-FIRST CENTURY

By the turn of the twenty-first century, the Smith's trustees had sold much of the landed property that had been in the ownership of the estate and these endowments are now held in stocks and shares. Of the original estates, only Longney, Thurlaston and Warbleton now produce income for the charity – but the parish grants are now funded from the main investment fund. With such a reduction in landholdings, the work of Cluttons (the London company as well as the one in East Grinstead – for the charity maintained its long connection with both) is no longer central to its operations; the legal firm of Warrens, once Bray's, which appears on so much of the correspondence of two centuries, is also no longer engaged with the day-to-day running of the charity, though it is still involved.

A new Scheme, in 2000, revisited the traditional criteria for allocations and also gave the trustees the power to decide on precisely how much the parishes would receive from the estate. This raised the grants considerably (before this the sums had sometimes been so small that parishes had refused them): in 2008, the minimum a parish could receive as a grant was £1,575. Instructions were that local parish trustees would give priority to 'the relief of poor, aged or infirm persons or in advancing in life such persons' and to hospitals or convalescent homes.

Peter Crook, who lives in the large village of Great Bookham, Surrey, is the treasurer of the Bookham United Trust (which covers several local grants including Henry Smith's); the charity is marked up on a board in the church of St Nicholas in the village. The board of local trustees meets to study applications for help (and detailed accounts of those successful will be filed by him to make sure that they can claim next year's grant). 'We are looking at cases of need in today's environment,' says Peter Crook. They work too with local health professionals and the social services – and these occasionally refer potential applicants to the trustees. 'Last week', he said in an interview, 'we were able to give assistance to a single mother with two children. In order that she can work, we will cover some extra playgroup costs.' Sometimes they help with the costs of prams, cots and pushchairs, sometimes with payment for the costs of pre-school or for participation in school trips or camps. Great Bookham is in what appears to be a broadly affluent stretch of Surrey but Peter Crook says there are always 'pockets of need behind the scenes'.

Those kindred who are needy are still given

A VISITOR'S STORY

Since the 1980s, the charity has maintained a taskforce of volunteer visitors whose job it is to visit and summarise for the trustees those projects that have applied for grants. Maggie Hill has been a visitor since 2005. She makes on average just over a visit a month, most of them in the Brighton area where she lives, and all of them on the basis of an application that has already been passed through the trustees and various screening processes in the Henry Smith office. Having made her visit, Maggie then submits a confidential report to the trustees – 'I'm NOT a decision maker,' she stresses – but nonetheless, the visitors are an important stage of the final process for any project hoping for a grant.

Like all the visitors, Maggie is looking for evidence that projects are well governed and that their numbers make sense – as well as something more elusive that indicates a project is in good health. She loves the work, she says: 'I get to meet a wide range of people and I'm in a position to actually help.'

On this page and p. 119 are shown a selection of the many projects that have been helped in recent years by grants from the Henry Smith Charity. *Clockwise from top left:* The Food Chain; Wombourne Special Needs Support Group; Action Medical Research; St Giles Trust; Taw and Torridge CVS; Greenhouse Schools' Project; Demand.

assistance – and Henry might be surprised by how many (nearly 6,000) are now registered with the charity. Nominations for the poor clergy fund now come from the diocesan offices – and the reasons given for nominations over the last decade are still varied: for one clergyman the costs of a wood-burning stove, for example, in a cold vicarage; for another, help towards a flight to New Zealand for a clergyman's wife who needs to visit her dying mother; for another; help with the cost of a stairlift for a seriously ill spouse.

The range of the Henry Smith Charity's grant-giving has extended far beyond anything (and anywhere) that could possibly have been envisaged by Henry himself or by Richard Amherst, George Whitmore, William Rolfe or by any of the first trustees. Yet the current charity remains as true to the spirit of those original bequests as is possible in such a different world. The one bequest that seems now particularly archaic, the money to be used for the redemption of the captives of Barbary pirates, has found an outlet that is both modern and completely timeless. People are still held captive – and in Britain they are working as modern-day slave domestics or trafficked into prostitution.

Zaiba Qureshi of Housing for Women runs the Re-Place project in Brixton, providing temporary housing for women who have been trafficked from all over the world into prostitution in the United Kingdom. The charity, which has grown out of a housing association, saw that there was a need to fill the gap between the safe houses to which women were protected when they first escaped and the next stage, which is applying for asylum (all the residents of Re-Place come from outside Europe) and trying to prepare for independent living. There is no going back to their original country for most of these women – in many cases they have been trafficked by their own relatives and in others the fear of being seen as disgraced makes it impossible: they are in effect exiled.

Re-Place offers self-contained accommodation, flats or bedsits, which see them through this difficult period, providing counselling, legal advice and support with learning English or useful skills. Six years after Re-Place was set up, Zaiba described in an interview how resilient the residents are: one woman is studying for a degree in fashion and several more are keen to train as carers. Fundraising for the project was not easy, it is a subject that often 'doesn't pull heart-strings', but three years of funding from the Henry Smith Charity helped get it underway.

In Leeds, the Anneli Project provides another refuge for trafficked women, their temporary (six to twelve months) accommodation filling in the often frightening space between rescue and independent living. Kate Bratt-Farrar of Leeds Women's Aid described how the project had to address the very different needs of the women, how they often had addiction problems, how they had no recourse to public funds and were fearful of seeking help, as they might be sent to the police; many women were trafficked as children. One woman, found by police in a brothel, had not had her hair touched for years and it was matted and tangled. One of the first things that the Anneli Project brought in was a hairdresser – not only to help restore her self-worth but also to offer her a glimpse of a free life.

Elsewhere too the charity has funded projects that help restore people to mainstream life. At Homestart in Sheffield, for example, parents and families, often isolated, get visits from befriending volunteers who are there to talk, to help play with the children or simply to offer some encouragement, a much-needed show of friendship and support. The Henry Smith Charity has funded Homestart's learning and development project for pre-school-age children – giving parents the tools and the confidence to be 'first teachers'. Their offices are lined with boxes that can be used as rattles, interestingly textured materials that can be explored and fun games to be made out of old packets.

Henry Smith, as far as we know, never went to Wales, but the charity reaches there now – with a programme of grants. In rural Carmarthenshire, the Pencader community centre has become a focal point in a region where there is high unemployment and poverty. The centre, in an old stone building, runs a food co-op, a thriving savings' scheme and a play-

Clockwise from top left: Megan Baker House; Julian House; Grand Central Savings; Coming Together in Woodhouse Little London; Reach Community Projects; Quaker Social Action; Just for Kids Law.

group; there are storytelling sessions and day-trips and it offers isolated mothers the company of others. It is a very inspiring place, full of warmth and energy. Henry Smith would surely have wholeheartedly approved of the way that just by being there, Pencader helps to restore to a fragmented community a confidence in its own possibilities.

In Edinburgh is a L'Arche house – one of the visionary communities started by Jean Vanier over 50 years ago and now found all over the world. In L'Arche homes, people with intellectual disabilities live alongside fellow residents, carers and volunteers in terms of total equality. John Redwood, the community leader, describes the L'Arche ethos as truly a 'shared life'. 'The emphasis here is on mutual relationships, having real friendships that are reciprocal – not just based on paid care. We look at issues such as the quality of welcome we give to people and respect – we take care always to celebrate people's birthdays.' Residents of L'Arche have a home for life and now in Edinburgh they are looking at ways of imaginatively thinking about old age, at a community specifically for residents who develop dementia. Their new shared living project is a cluster of flats, occupied by four individuals, of whom two are relatively able and independent – this offers a different style of community for those who prefer to live independently but with the underpinning of support that being part of L'Arche gives.

Our researches into the life of Henry Smith have demonstrated to a remarkable degree the power both of change and continuity over the centuries. The Archbishop of Canterbury still approves new trustees, as laid down by the Attorney General in 1626. The descendants of Joan Jackson are looked after by the charity as its founder wanted. The Church of England, less than a century old when Henry Smith made his will, is still recognised in the poor clergy fund. The threat of Barbary pirates may have gone but slavery is still a reality recognised in the grants made by the charity. The parishes selected by those first trustees, deal-making Jacobeans like Henry himself, still receive an annual sum that goes to help those in need. Over the years the charity has adapted to the changes and requirements of each age. But it has never lost sight of the mission laid down by its founder, which was to use its substantial assets to relieve poverty and want and to promote human flourishing.

Henry Smith would not recognise the Henry Smith Charity as it exists today; he would certainly be amazed by the Britain in which it still operates and the multifarious ways in which need is both defined and how it is relieved – represented by the many thousands of projects that have been funded by the charity. Yet he would surely also be delighted to see that the years spent obsessively planning his legacy in the 1620s were not for nothing. Henry wanted his fortune to be put to good use – and 350 years later, with £27 million a year to give away, it is still doing so.

A farm on the Longney estate in Gloucestershire in 2014. The estate was purchased by Henry Smith in 1602 and still belongs to the Henry Smith Charity.

Notes

Abbreviations used in the Notes:

HSC	Henry Smith Charity
LMA	London Metropolitan Archive
PRO	Public Record Office
SHC	Surrey History Centre
TNA	The National Archives
VCH	Victoria County History

1. The pedigree, drawn up by Charles Perkins Gwilt, is printed in–'Descent of Henry Smith, Esq., alderman of London', *Gentleman's Magazine*, vol. 107, pt 1 (1837), pp. 149–51
2. TNA, C3/159/83
3. TNA, PROB 11/173, fols 103v–105
4. The archive of the Salters' Company
5. TNA, C2/CHASI/A32/66
6. Court of Common Council, City Record Office
7. Quoted in Claire Cross, *The Puritan Earl: the life of Henry Hastings, third Earl of Huntingdon, 1536–1595*, 1966, p. 89
8. TNA, C78/111/6
9. TNA, C78/111/6
10. Quoted in I. M. Calder, *Activities of the Puritan faction of the Church of England, 1625–33*, London, 1957, p. 79
11. Longleat House, Devereux papers, DE box 9, no. 151
12. Quoted in Calder, *Activities*, p. 79
13. HSC archive
14. TNA, PROB 11/327, fols 67v–68r
15. N. E. McClure (ed.), *The Letters of John Chamberlain*, Michigan, 1962, vol. 2, p. 551
16. HSC archive: Richard Lumley's response
17. Calder, *Activities*, p. 63
18. PRO, C2/CHAS/A32/66
19. PRO 11/153/55
20. Joseph Gwilt sketched a family tree that connected the Phelips line with the Smiths on a blank page of his copy of William Bray's *Collections*, now in the library of the Society of Antiquaries.
21. Manor of Esher Waterville, KF2, Kingston Museum and Heritage Service
22. TNA, PROB 11/160/481
23. TNA, PROB 11/240, fols 402r–403v
24. From *England's Comfort and London's Joy: Expressed in the Royall, Triumphant and Magnificent Entertainment of our Dread Soveraigne Lord, King Charles, at his blessed and safe returne from Scotland, 25 November 1641, by John Taylor*, London, 1641
25. TNA, PROB 11/201, fols 460r–465v
26. TNA, C78/489/20
27. TNA, C2/CHAS I/B77/56; C2/CHAS I/B66/11; C2/CHAS I/B107/62; C2/CHAS I/B115/12; C2/CHAS I/B78/2; C2/CHAS I/B157/52
28. W/D/112/1, Oxfordshire Health Archives
29. D2455/T2/2/2/4, Gloucestershire Archives

30. Hare 989/190, Norfolk Record Office
31. Lawrence Stone, *The Crisis of the Aristocracy, 1558–1641*, Oxford, 1965, p. 341
32. W. H. Rylands (ed.), *The Four Visitations of Berkshire*, Harleian Society, 1907–8, vols 56 and 57
33. Calendar of State Papers Domestic (Berkshire), 1629–31 (1860), p. 276
34. Calendar of State Papers Domestic (Berkshire), 1660–1 (1860), p. 32
35. TNA, PROB 11/214 fols 332v-333r
36. *A History of the County of Surrey*, VCH, vol. 3, pp. 72–7
37. TNA, PROB 11/173, fols 103v–105
38. TNA, PROB 11/161, fols 486v–487v
39. TNA, C2/CHASI/A32/66
40. TNA, C2/CHASI/A32/66
41. SHC, P41/6/3A
42. PRO C10/30/37
43. Keith Wrightson and David Levine, *Poverty and Piety in an English Village: Terling, 1525–1700*, 2nd edn, Oxford, 1995
44. Wrightson and Levine, *Poverty and Piety*, p. 222
45. TNA, C54/3995, Chancery Close Roll 1658
46. F. H. W. Sheppard (ed.), *Southern Kensington: Brompton*, Survey of London, 41, 1983, pp. 83–129
47. HSC archive: 3 Feb. 26 Charles II [i.e. 3 February 1663/64], Order for Additional Trustees for Surrey
48. SHC 2414/4/2
49. HSC archive
50. *The Case and Justification of Sir John Pettus, of the county of Suffolk, Knight*, London, 1677–8, pp. 1–3.
51. HSC archive
52. Lambeth Palace Library, MSS 933, no. 80
53. *A General Report of the Agriculture of Surrey*, 1794, quoted in VCH, *Surrey*, pp. 438–9
54. *Wimbledon Vestry Minutes, 1736, 1743–1788*, Surrey Record Society, 1964, vol. 25, p. 24
55. Quoted in Steve Hindle, *On the Parish*, London, 2004, p. 205
56. Quoted in H. A. Walter, *A Short History of Reigate Grammar School, 1675–1975*, Reigate, 1975, p. 18
57. William Bray, *Collections Relating to Henry Smith, Esq., some time Alderman of London*, London, 1800, p. 31
58. Christopher Baugh, 'Michael Novosielski', Oxford Dictionary of National Biography, 2004
59 LMA P71/TMS/0541
60 Quoted in Malcolm Thick, *The Neat House Gardens: Early Market Gardening Around London*, Totnes, 1998, p. 59
61. Private memorandum, Kenneth Marr-Johnson (26 March 1968), HSC archive
62. LMA P95/MRY1/504/1–9
63. HSC archive

Selected Bibliography of Published Sources

Our researches drew on the only two previously published accounts of the life of Henry Smith and the early years of Smith's Charity. William Bray's *Collections Relating to Henry Smith, Esq., some time Alderman of London; the Estates by Him given to Charitable Uses; and the Trustees Appointed by Him* was published in 1800 and Charles Perkins Gwilt's *Notices Relating to Thomas Smith of Campden and to Henry Smith, Sometime Alderman of London* in 1826.

We gleaned a great deal of information from the Victoria County History series, particularly the volumes on Surrey and London, the *Oxford Dictionary of Biography* and *The History of Parliament*, vols 1558-1603, 1604-1629, 1640-1660 and 1660–1690.

Among many other sources, we consulted the following:

Archer, Ian, *The pursuit of Stability: Social Relations in Elizabethan London*, Cambridge, 1991

Barty-King, Hugh, *The Salters' Company 1394-1994*, London, 1994

Beaven, Alfred B, *The Aldermen of the City of London. Temp. Henry III-1908*, London, 1908

Boulton, Jeremy, *Neighbourhood and Society: a London suburb in the Seventeenth Century*, Cambridge, 1987

Colley, Linda, *Captives: Britain, Empire and the World, 1600-1850*, London, 2003

Cowe, F. M. (ed.), *Wimbledon Vestry Minutes*, Surrey Record Society, 1964

Dale, T. C., *The Inhabitants of London in 1638*, London, 1931

Drew, Charles (ed.), *Lambeth Churchwardens' Accounts, 1504-1645 and vestry book, 1641*, Surrey Record Society, 1950

Eden, Frederick Morton, *The State of the Poor: A Facsimile of the 1797 Edition*, London, 1966

Faulkner, Thomas, *History and Antiquities of Kensington*, London, 1820

Hindle, Steve, *On the Parish: The Micro-Politics of Poor Relief in Rural England, 1550-1750*, 2004

Jones, Nicholas, *God and the Moneylenders: Usury and the Law in Early Modern England*, Oxford, 1989.

Jordan, W. K., *Philanthropy in England, 1480-1660: A Study of the Changing Patterns of English Aspiration*, Abingdon, 1959

Mingay, G. E. (ed.), *Arthur Young and His Times*, London, 1975

Nicolls, Charles, *The Lodger: Shakespeare on Silver Street*, London, 2007

Noyes, Ann, *Shere Poverty: From Parish Workhouse to Union Workhouse*, Surrey, 1996

Picard, Liza, *Everyday Life in Elizabethan London*, London, 2004

Rappaport, Steve, *Worlds within Worlds: Structures of Life Within Sixteenth Century London*, 1989

Sackville-West, Robert, *Inheritance: The Story of Knole and the Sackvilles*, London, 2010

Stow, John, *Survey of London*, London, 1598 (1956 edition)

Stroud, Dorothy, *The South Kensington Estate of Henry Smith's Charity: its history and development*, London, 1975

Styles, John, *The Dress of the People: Everyday Fashion in Eighteenth Century England*, London, 2007

Underdown, David, *Fire from Heaven: Life in an English town in the Seventeenth Century*, London, 1992

Wales, Tim, 'Poverty, poor-relief and the life-cycle: some evidence from seventeenth-century Norfolk' in R. M. Smith (ed.), *Land, Kinship and Life-Cycle*, Cambridge, 1984, pp. 351-404

Ward, W. E. (ed.), *Parson and parish in Eighteenth-Century Hampshire*, Hampshire Records Series, vol. 13, 1995

Ward, W. R. (ed.), *Parson and Parish in Eighteenth-Century Surrey: Replies to bishops' visitations*, Surrey Record Office, 1994

Wrightson, Keith, and Levine, David, *Poverty and Piety in an English Village: Terling, 1525-1700*, Oxford, 1995

Parishes Supported by the Estates Fund

Parishes supported by the Estates Fund, as of 2006, grouped according to the Estates with which they were historically associated. Parishes marked with an asterisk are no longer in the scheme. Parishes marked + are now grouped as one.

Bexhill Estate

Addington
Beddington
Bermondsey & St Thomas
Carshalton*
Caterham
Chaldon
Chelsham
Clapham
Limpsfield*
Merton
Mitcham*
Morden*
St George the Martyr, Southwark
St Olave, Southwark*
St Saviour, Southwark
Sanderstead*
Sutton
Titsey*
Tooting
Warlingham (now grouped with Chelsham)
Woldingham*
Woodmansterne

Eastbrooke Estate

Bisley
Byfleet
Chobham
Egham
Esher
Long Ditton
Pyrford
Stoke d'Abernon
Thames Ditton
Thorpe
Weybridge*

Iwood Estate

Chertsey
Cobham
East Molesey St Mary
East Molesey St Paul*
Effingham
Great Bookham
Leatherhead
Little Bookham
Petersham, Richmond
Walton-on-Thames
West Molesey

Kempsing Estate

Barnes
Battersea
Camberwell
Lambeth
Mortlake
Newington
Putney
Richmond (also linked with Tellescombe Estate)
Rotherhithe
St Thomas, Southwark* (also linked with Longney Estate)
Streatham (also linked with Longney Estate)
Wimbledon

Longney Estate

Batheaston
Calne
Chediston
Chippenham
Chipping Barnet
Christchurch, Newgate Street+
Horne (also linked with Worth Estate)
Kings Langley
Longney
Newton St Loe
Northill
Odiham
Ormskirk
New Radnor
Pershore
St Giles, Cripplegate
St Luke, Old Street (also linked with Thurlaston Estate)
St Martin-in-the-Fields
St Olave, Old Jewry+
St Sepulchre (City)+
St Sepulchre (Middlesex)
St Thomas, Southwark*
St Vedast, Foster Lane+
Stanton Prior
Streatham
Warbleton

Longstock Estate

Broughton
Charlton
Chester-le-Street
Dorking
Gateshead
Harting
Haslemere
Hesledon (now linked with Murton)
Longstock
Ludgershall*
Lumley
Murton
Singleton (now linked with Charlton)
Stoughton (now linked with Walderton)
Walderton
Westbourne
Winkfield

Tellescombe Estate

Banbury*
Chobham*
Culkerton
Henley
Richmond*
Southampton*

Thurlaston Estate

Andover
Bedworth
Bledlow*
Broad Hinton
Dovercourt
East Dereham
East Grinstead
Ramsey
Reigate
St Botolph, Aldersgate+
St Giles, Cripplegate*
St Luke, Old Street*
St John in Bedwardine
St John, Chester (now linked with St Michael, Chester)
St Michael, Chester
St Sepulchre (City)+
St Sepulchre (Middlesex)*
Shapwick*
Thetford
Wandsworth
Warminster
Waterbeach
Westbury

Warbleton Estate

Albury
Alfold
Ash
Bramley
Capel
Chiddingfold
Compton
Cranleigh
Dunsfold
East Clandon*
East Horsley
Elstead
Farleigh (now grouped with Chelsham)
Frensham
Frimley
Hambledon
Hascombe
Haslemere*
Horsell
Malden
Merrow
Ockham
Peperharow
Pirbright
Puttenham
Seale
Send & Ripley
Shalford
Shottermill
Stoke Next Guildford (now linked with Merrow)
Thursley
West Clandon
West Horsley
Windlesham
Wisley*
Witley
Woking
Wonersh
Worplesdon

Worth Estate

Abinger
Ashtead
Banstead
Betchworth
Bletchingley
Buckland
Burstow
Charlwood
Cheam
Chessington
Chipstead
Coulsdon
Crowhurst
Epsom
Ewell
Ewhurst
Gatton*
Godstone
Headley
Horley
Horne
Leigh
Lingfield
Merstham
Mickleham
Newdigate
Nutfield
Ockley
Oxted
Shere
Tandridge
Walton-on-the-Hill
Wotton

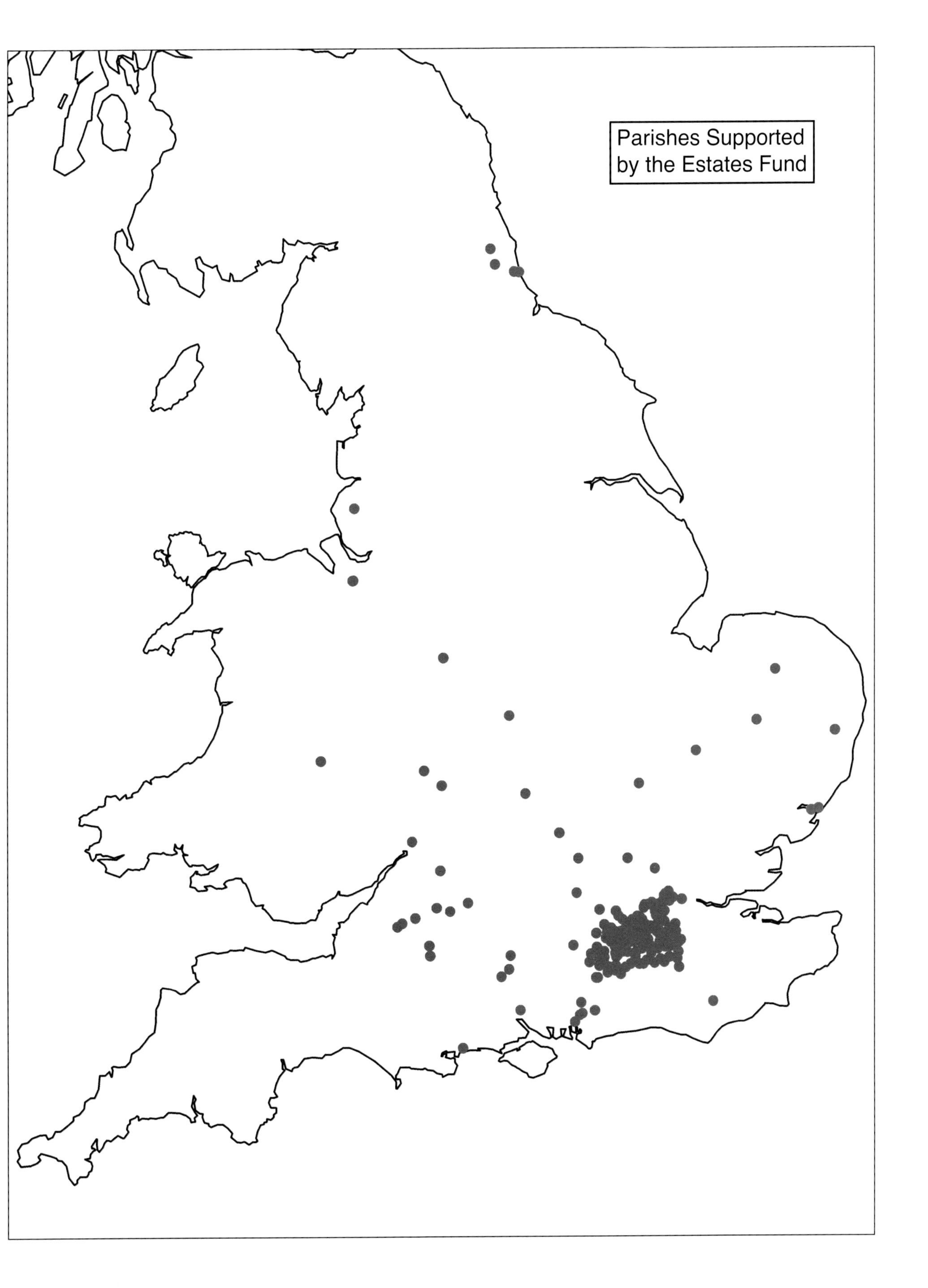
Parishes Supported
by the Estates Fund

List of Grants

General and Special grants made by the Henry Smith Charity 1910–2010 adjusted for inflation to show the 2013 equivalent (using the converter tool on the Bank of England website)

Year	*Grants*	*2013 equivalent*
	£	£
1910	9,700	996,978
1920	15,500	604,500
1930	30,575	1,743,835
1940	43,050	2,102,843
1950	30,000	897,000

Year	*Grants*	*2013 equivalent*
	£	£
1960	43,000	864,116
1970	210,000	2,834,569
1980	2,000,000	7,483,504
1990	8,350,000	16,560,693
2000	22,880,000	33,604,787
2010	21,656,000	24,229,476

These are the grants made in the last year of each decade, originally to hospitals and then to the Charity's wider objects as these were sanctioned by the Charity Commissioners. They do not include grants made to kindred, parishes or poor clergy.

Modern Money Equivalents

Modern money equivalents, showing suggested rounded values. For example £10 in 1627 would be roughly equivalent to £2,300 in today's money.

	£1,000	£100	£10
1627	230,000	23,000	2,300
1753	195,000	19,500	1,950
1868	100,000	10,000	1,000
1950	30,000	3,025	303

Modern money equivalents calculated using *Consumer Price Inflation since 1750* by O'Donoghue, Goulding and Allen (2004); *Economic Trends*, March 2004, pp. 38–46; and *Seven Centuries of the Prices of Consumables* by Phelps-Brown and Hopkins (1956), pp. 311–14.

Picture Acknowledgements

The publisher would like to thank the following individuals, galleries and institutions for permission to reproduce their illustrations. Every care has been taken to trace copyright holders. However, if we have omitted anyone we apologise and will, if informed, make corrections in any future edition.

Key BAL = Bridgeman Art Library, London

RBK & C = The Royal Borough of Kensington & Chelsea Local Studies & Archives, London

The numbers below are page numbers.

Endpapers. British Library, London/BAL

Frontispiece. All Saints Church, Wandsworth/Dr John Crook

Title page. Reproduced by permission of Surrey History Centre, Woking

xi. The Henry Smith Charity, London/Dr John Crook

xii. UCL Art Museum, University College, London/BAL

2. Private Collection/© Look and Learn/Peter Jackson Collection/BAL

3. All Saints Church, Wandsworth/Dr John Crook

5. St James's Church, Chipping Campden/Dr John Crook

6. Private Collection/BAL

7. By kind permission of the Salters' Company, London/Mitzi de Margary

8. Private Collection/BAL

9. By permission of the Folger Shakespeare Library, Washington D.C., U.S.A.

10. Anne of Cleves House, Lewes, courtesy of Sussex Archaeological Society

11. Dr John Crook

12. Private Collection

13. Private Collection/BAL

14. By permission of the Pepys Library, Magdalene College, Cambridge

15. British Museum, London/BAL

17 above & below. Dr John Crook

18. Kenwood House, London/© English Heritage Photo Library/BAL

19. Victoria & Albert Museum, London/BAL

21. Knole House, Sevenoaks/John Bethell/BAL

25. © National Portrait Gallery, London

28. All Saints Church, Wandsworth/Dr John Crook

29. All Saints Church, Wandsworth/Dr John Crook

30. The National Archive, Kew/Tim Wales

31. Kedleston Hall, Derbyshire/The National Trust

33. © National Portrait Gallery, London

34. Private Collection/BAL

37. Private Collection/BAL

38. Private Collection/BAL

39. The Royal Collection © 2011 Her Majesty Queen Elizabeth II/BAL

41. By kind permission of the Haberdashers' Company, London

43. Private Collection/BAL

49. Waterstock Church, Oxfordshire/Dr John Crook

50. Private Collection/BAL

51. The old church of St Peter and St Paul, Albury/by kind permission of The Churches Conservation Trust/Dr John Crook

52. London Metropolitan Archives, © City of London

53. Holy Trinity Church, Guildford/Dr John Crook

55. All Saints Church, Wandsworth/Dr John Crook

57. London Metropolitan Archives, © City of London/ Tim Wales

58. Reproduced by permission of Surrey History Centre, Woking/Tim Wales

61. Fitzwilliam Museum, University of Cambridge/BAL

62. Private Collection/BAL

63. © Tokyo Fuji Art Museum, Tokyo, Japan/BAL

65. Pershore Abbey, Worcestershire/Dr John Crook

66. British Library, London/BAL

67. Dr John Crook

69. Museum of London

70. Private Collection/© Look and Learn/Elgar Collection/BAL

71. By kind permission of RBK & C

72. Yale Center for British Art, Paul Mellon Collection, U.S.A./BAL

74. © National Portrait Gallery, London

77. Yale Center for British Art, Gift of Paul Mellon, U.S.A./BAL

78. Surrey Heath Museum, Camberley

79. Yale Center for British Art, Paul Mellon Collection, U.S.A./BAL

81. Dr John Crook

83. By kind permission of Peter Harrington Books, London

84. Private Collection/BAL

85. Reproduced by permission of Lambeth Archives Department, London

86. Wellcome Library, London

87. © Scottish National Gallery, Edinburgh/BAL

88. The Henry Smith Charity, London

89. Private Collection, by courtesy of Surrey History Centre, Woking

90 above. Private Collection, by courtesy of RH & RW Clutton

90 below. By courtesy of RH & RW Clutton/Dr John Crook

91. © National Portrait Gallery, London

93. Private Collection/BAL

94. All Saints Church, Wandsworth/Dr John Crook

97. Yale Center for British Art, Paul Mellon Collection, U.S.A./BAL

99. Private Collection/BAL

100. By kind permission of RBK & C

101. By kind permission of RBK & C

102 above & below. The Henry Smith Charity, on loan to the RIBA Drawings Collection, London, photographs © RIBA

103. Private Collection/© Look and Learn/Peter Jackson Collection/BAL

104 above & below. By kind permission of RBK & C

105. Private Collection/© Look and Learn/Peter Jackson Collection,BAL

106. Private Collection

107. By kind permission of RBK & C

108. By kind permission of RBK & C

109. By kind permission of All About Kids

111. Amoret Tanner Collection/The Art Archive, London

112. Private Collection/Photo © Christie's Images/ BAL

113. By kind permission of RBK & C

114. London Metropolitan Archives © City of London/reproduced by kind permission of Mrs Dennis Flanders

117. The Henry Smith Charity, London

119. The Henry Smith Charity, London

120. Dr John Crook

Index

LONDON.